the **Spontaneous**

YOU

the Spontaneous YOU

Norman Grubb

CHRISTIAN LITERATURE CRUSADE
Fort Washington, Pennsylvania 19034

CHRISTIAN LITERATURE CRUSADE

U.S.A.
Box 1449, Fort Washington, Pennsylvania 19034

CANADA
Box 189, Elgin, Ontario KOG 1EO

GREAT BRITAIN
51 The Dean, Alresford, Hants., SO24 9BJ

AUSTRALIA
P. O. Box 91, Pennant Hills, N.S.W. 2120

First published 1966
First American edition 1981
This printing 1985

ISBN 0-87508-224-6

PRINTED IN THE UNITED STATES OF AMERICA

Contents

Foreword

I DON'T KNOW how I came to make writing on these lines the pursuit of my latter years—but it has been. Moving on in earlier years from seeking and finding the answer to my personal problems, it seemed as if my mind awakened to the need of finding and understanding the answer to "the riddle of the universe", at least in terms of our human participation in it.

I began to ask three questions: What is life? How do we live it? Why do we live it? And I began to find that there is an answer. With the guide lines of the Scriptures, with the insights of some of the great See-ers of history, Jacob Boehme, William Law, Soren Kierkegaard and others (and sometimes also catching beams of light from the more unorthodox), my first attempt at putting what I saw into writing was an unpublished pamphlet which I called *The Dark and Light Principle*. Perhaps that had more of the fire of first discoveries, though not always in temperate terms. Then followed, nineteen years ago and in succeeding years, *The Law of Faith*, *The Liberating Secret*, *The Deep Things of God*, and *God Unlimited*, all of which are still in circulation. Each has been an attempt at going a little further into sharing with others what have become pearls of great price to me. Some have found *The Law of Faith* clarifying on the subject of how theory becomes experience, others the key to the released personality in *The Liberating Secret*. *The Deep Things of God* has been an attempt to dig into the law of opposites, an understanding of which puts so many of the puzzles of life into focus: Blake's "Build a heaven in hell's despair". To my mind, and by the evidence of readers' comments *God Unlimited* has been the clearest and most comprehensive of all, and should be, as the whole panorama of God and man comes clearer, like surveying a landscape from a high mountain.

This present book has been written at the suggestion of my old friend, Abraham Vereide, the founder of International Christian Leadership, which sponsors the Presidential Prayer Breakfasts held annually in Washington, and many other like events on state and city levels, with its call to a leadership led by God. (I had the privilege of writing his biography also, entitled *Modern Viking*.)

I seek again in this book to dig down into the foundations and examine the basis of human living, not as a theory but in workable experience. It said in the book of the Acts that Aquila and Priscilla took "a certain Jew named Apollos . . . and expounded unto him the way of God more perfectly". I like that. We can leave out the "more perfectly", but every time I speak with a group or in a public meeting, or talk things over with the hundreds eager to find the really releasing answer to living free in their private prisons of frustrating circumstances, it is a going over and over again and a further clarifying of this broad, free highway, on which we can drive with confidence, as it were, the automobile of our daily living—and with zest and pleasure, and find the purpose in it not for ourselves but others. That is why I use this title of *The Spontaneous You*. It is not original. I wrote an article for that living magazine, *Christian Life*, and my friend the Editor,

Robert Walker, gave it this title. So I asked him permission to use it again for this book, which he kindly granted.

The older I get, the more I recognize what I owe to God's priceless gift to me through these forty-five years of my wife, Pauline, the daughter of C. T. Studd to whom I refer in later pages, who in oneness of heart and mind provides the home life which makes writing like this so much easier. I also thank the Publishers, Lutterworth Press, who have for the past thirty years never turned down anything I have offered them—and that takes faith and grace! And the Christian Literature Crusade who take on the distribution in the United States.

NORMAN P. GRUBB

Fort Washington,
Pennsylvania, U.S.A.

CHAPTER I

Modern Man and the Ultimate Question

I AM GREATLY interested in the inward direction of our thinking these days, which is causing so much religious ferment. It seems to be giving the skeptic cause to say, "Where is your God up there? We can do without these external religious forms and the dogmas of a distant Deity. We have our answers to our human enigmas: they are within, not without."

Of course, we know the "natural man" always has said and will say that kind of thing, whereas the man of the Spirit knows another dimension which includes the within and without. But taking him on his own ground, there is a direction in modern discoveries which does emphatically point inward, but which, so far from making irrelevant the "faith once delivered to the saints", brings it so sharply into focus that it alone is the final answer. We will start from there.

It is true that in area after area of human life, where in the past we had no complete explanation of the working of things, we now find the answer within. Most exciting of all has been the mystery of the composition of matter. Of what does it consist? The schoolboy now knows that (to use the language of the amateur) within matter is the molecule, within the molecule the atom, within the atom the nucleus, within the nucleus illimitable energy.

Then what about the body? Where is the key to

physical life? The answer again is within—in the cell, the genes, or whatever their correct names are, to the point that some claim that physical life will soon be reproduced in a test tube.

Then the mind? Are mental conditions due to outside influences? Now we probe within, the psychologists explore the subconscious, the unconscious, the doctors investigate the brain cells. Even in our social relationships, we no longer accept the imposition from without of "the divine right of kings", or "the rich man in his castle, the poor man at his gate", as if some by birth, race, or colour are inferior people. We seek for the answer within and among us in the right of every man to an equal opportunity.

It is true that our answers are being found within—within—within: and that brings us directly to our final inner problem—ourselves as humans, the human personality, the individual self. And here we are stopped short. We meet the insoluble to which no one on a merely human level has found the answer. We all agree—all philosophies and religions have said the same thing through the centuries—that if we humans have not a nature that is naturally loving and to the point that we genuinely are as concerned for the welfare of our neighbor as for ourselves, then the life of the human race, with all its boasted developments, can never be more than a patched-up affair and can be lived at best under some forms of external control. We have never known and do not know by what means this final inner citadel of man can be captured, and self-loving man become naturally self-giving man. We are beaten at the center.

If, therefore, there is some inmost fact about us humans which is missing, and which could put us on to the right track, what is it? Here is precisely where there always has been the answer, and an inward answer—but not in man. Here it is, and always has been—in the Bible. Paul put it in one word which he stated to be the hidden secret of the universe which always had been known to the initiated, but had only now come into public view. He called it "the mystery which had been hid from ages and generations but now is made manifest . . . " The trouble was that it has been so overlaid by external religious forms and symbols that what was really an internal truth—an inner relationship—had been given the image of an approach to an external and distant person—to God "up there" rather than God "in here".

CHAPTER 2

No Foundation, No Building

J ESUS MADE THE ultimate statement when he told the woman of Samaria, a simple woman of her day and no profound philosopher, "God is Spirit". We understand what a spirit is in Biblical terms, because we are human spirits, for the writer to the Hebrews called God "the Father of spirits". The Bible definition of a spirit is the inner self—as Paul says, "What man knoweth the things of a man save the spirit of man which is in him?" The spirit is the I, whether of God or man, which can only say of itself, "I am". It cannot be described, it can only be affirmed. We are—that is all we can say. But the important point is that this inner ego, which is I, is invisible, unreachable, meaningless, unless joined to me as part of me there is also means of expressing my "I". Therefore, we humans have, as spontaneous parts of ourselves, our souls (our emotions and reasons), and our bodies. They are not actually ourselves, they are our means of self-expression, yet they are so much parts of ourselves that we function as a spontaneous unity.

So with God. The Bible from the beginning reveals him as "The Universal Spirit", The One Person in the universe ("beside me there is no other"), who is also invisible, unapproachable and meaningless except to Himself, unless He has His means of expression. The Bible shows that the universe is His means of expression.

The second verse of the Bible says, "The Spirit moved upon the face of the waters", and lo, the creation.

That means that we must recognize Him as the world's Creator in a different relationship from the way we regard, for instance, a carpenter and the chairs he makes. We humans make things, but are separate from the things we make. But we have to learn not to attribute the limitations of our three-dimensional thinking—length, breadth, height—to the dimensionless One with whom there is no such thing as space and time, as here and there. With Him, therefore, we are to see that He *is* the things He makes; they are the forms He takes, in the same ways as our bodies are we, and yet not we. He is to be seen in the atom, in the tree, in music, colour, everything; as Browning says, "God is seen God in the star, in the stone, in the flesh, in the soul and the clod." When I look at a person, I don't differentiate between him and his body, though I know that actually he is not his body. So with God.

The important thing is to begin to see Him, the Spirit, as the Within One, rather than the Without One (though He is that also). Open our eyes and everything is actually He manifesting Himself in one form or another. Not some things which He makes and should be regarded as apart from, like a carpenter. When we see this, we begin to see that there is only One Person in the universe.

We shall not get the world or the universe, or ourselves with our human problems into focus until we have settled in to the consciousness that there is only One Person in the universe; and all things and people find their place and meaning as derivatives and manifestations of Him, whether negatively or positively. Exactly as the Scriptures say of Him: "In him we live and move and have our being", He "fills all things", "God all in all", and Paul, that the non-Christian is without excuse because the visible things manifest the Godhead of the Invisible One.

But Spirit is person. We are spirits, we are persons, and personality in its freedom, originality, endless potential, can obviously not express itself through things, for things are limited, persons unlimited. How then can this One Person in the universe, God the Spirit, the Within One, express Himself? Obviously, by persons; and so we come to the Bible revelation of the meaning of the creation of persons. It is to be The Person through persons.

Human beings, therefore, are not fulfilling their destiny unless they are in a relationship in which we living is really He living by us. Anything less is really sub-human. But it must also be a relationship in which we are completely human persons, completely ourselves, not living by effort or compulsion, or law or dutiful obedience, but in a spontaneity in which we are we in all the full enjoyable expression of our humanity, and yet—so deep is the paradox—it is really He!

Turn to the Bible again, and we find it is exactly so. As far back as Joseph, a pagan monarch made the comment, "A man in whom the spirit of God is". Moses was told he was being given a successor "filled with the Spirit of God". David prayed in his great prayer of repentance, "Take not thy Holy Spirit from me", and "Uphold me with thy free Spirit". Years after, when David's Psalms were quoted in Hebrews, it spoke of the Spirit, "saying in (not to) David". Ezekiel said, "I will put my Spirit within you".

Peter gathered all the great men of the Old Covenant together under one comment, "The prophets inquired what or what manner of time the Spirit of Christ which was in them did signify . . . "; and Jesus, the Son, again spoke the final authoritative word. He had often spoken of His relationship to the Father, and that He was going to the Father. So the disciples very sensibly asked Him, "Show us the Father", obviously thinking in our dimensional terms that some vision would be given them of a Person outside them. But His answer clinched it, when He said that the relationship of deity to humanity is the The Person within a person, not without; for they would have no vision given them of an external person. If they saw Him, they saw the Father, and not because He was the Father, but because "the words I speak unto you, I speak not of myself, but the Father that dwelleth in me, he doeth the works".

Then He went straight on to say that it was good He was leaving them, because if they understood that far, they now localized God as within Him; whereas God who is the Spirit was coming to universalize Himself within millions of humans, starting with themselves. He had previously called God Spirit and now He was saying that the Holy Spirit would be in them—the same Person.

And that was what happened at Pentecost. There they exchanged their faulty concept of an external God for the inner fixed consciousness, which cannot be described in our third-dimensional language, but can only be experienced, of the God who is Spirit, fused with their spirit, Ego with ego, as one and yet two. The means by which a human has a "personal Pentecost" may vary; that is not the important point. The end is invariable—a consciousness, a fixed unchangeable relationship in experience of God and me as one person.

The apostolic letters, which we call the Epistles, wholly bear that out. Paul's constant theme was Christ in us, expressed specifically as a part of his message in the statement already referred to—"the mystery hid from ages and generations, but now made manifest . . . Christ in you"; and his own marvelously balanced definition (to which we shall make further reference) of humanity and deity in combined action—"Nevertheless I live, no, it is not I, it is Christ living in me; yet now it is I living, and living by the affirmation of that fact", to paraphrase his great Galatians 2:20.

John takes it even farther, for Paul tells us how to get there, and John then tells us what we are when we do get there. John says, "No man hath seen God at any time"; and at once with our separated outlook, our eyes go upward and we say, "No, we have not seen Him"; but John as good as says, "You have got it wrong, He is not up there. I am not talking of a vertical but a horizontal God. If we love one another, that is God dwelling in us and His love perfected in us". God is actually the love *between* us when we are just spontaneously loving one another without direct consciousness of Him at all. (I John 4:12).

What then matters is, if He is the One Person in the universe, what kind of Person is He? The Bible makes that plain. To the three-worded statement, "God is Spirit", we add John's "God is love". Then we can see, what we said at the beginning, how we humans are right to find life's answers within, not without; but how we are brought to a final full-stop, when we cannot solve the ultimate "within" problem of man himself, who is not love, and cannot and does not want to live by living for his brother.

We are rightly brought to a full stop, for we are here faced with the ultimate and only meaning of the existence of persons. It is exactly here that the true revelation of God and man makes the only ultimate sense and is the only answer; for God as being love means something very different from our watered-down version of love. We mean by love, "give some, but keep plenty". But God as love means that He really is other people. Love is living other people's lives, and that is the whole meaning of life, its purpose, its fun, its gaiety, its seriousness, its fulfilment.

This we look into more closely later on, but we can now see that if the Only Person in the universe is love of this kind, and if, being Spirit, the Within One, He has as His means of manifestation a human race living this same kind of life, spontaneously and delightedly through His unity with them, so that they also are love, then the last piece of the jigsaw puzzle of the human race is in place and the picture whole— every limitless development of our human potential at full stretch, yet all geared solely to me for my neighbor, my neighbor for me. God and his universe have then come home.

CHAPTER 3

Where Things Went Wrong, and Why

PERSONALITY IS FREEDOM, and if persons are the expression of The Person, it must be freedom through freedom. How can there be such a delicate relationship that humans are real humans, all retaining their individuality, all conscious of themselves in their choices and actions, and yet the Deity Himself is imaged through each? How can that be?

First, we must have the meaning of "freedom" in focus. We humans have played fast and loose with the word, as with many others which press us too hard. We tend to regard the word as meaning a dispensation to be and do anything. Not so. Freedom is a meaningless concept unless it is freedom to choose. If there was only one thing in the world, there would be no choice, and therefore no freedom. There would not be such a word. But freedom has as its firm base the responsibility of making intelligent choices, and right ones. Then, when we have made our choices, freedom has its limitless expression within the bounds of that choice.

So freedom is limitless potential, expressed within limited choice. Marriage would be a human illustration. A supposedly intelligent choice is made, and then all freedom in family living is expressed within the limits of that choice. A young man chooses a profession, and then within its boundaries puts all he has into the development of his calling.

The startling proof of this being the meaning of freedom is that it is stated to be true of God. We say He is unlimited. The Bible says He is limited. Paul speaks of God that cannot lie. The writer to the Hebrews says it is impossible for God to lie. Not that He does not lie or should not, or did not, but He cannot. Therefore there is something God cannot do. What does that mean? To lie is one form of self-centredness. It is preserving one's own interests at the expense of another. Therefore, it is saying God cannot be a self-seeker, self-lover, self-magnifier.

Why, if God is freedom? Because freedom means right choice and all activities as an expression of that choice; and it is here saying that from eternity that "choice" has been God's eternal nature. He "cannot" be a self-seeker. He can only be a self-giver. Everything He has ever thought or done is in some form of self-giving. There is nothing else in His nature for all eternity.

"The eternal will to all goodness", William Law calls Him, and His real life is not being Himself, but living the life of His creation. This is love and this is the Trinity—the invisible Father who took form in the Son, from whom the Spirit proceeds in reproduction and creation; and it is for this reason that everything has a trinitarian form. It is the Father—Son—Spirit in manifestation; space—length, breadth, height; time—past, present, future; matter—energy, motion, phenomena; action—thought, word, deed; man—spirit, soul, body; any living thing such as a tree—essence, form, reproduction. More than that, everything has God's character of self-giving love, though, of course, in an involuntary way; everything has its true life, not in being itself, but in becoming others or something to others: the tree becomes the chair and table: bread and meat become our body: water is our life. Everything is a servant, by giving up its independent life to become somebody else's life; and this is God.

So now back to us humans. We will ask again and answer again: If God is the one life of the universe, if He, the Trinity-in-unity, is self-giving love, if all the universe is really He manifesting Himself in various forms and on various levels, what are we humans?

The answer is clear. God, the Living Person, in the free expression of His self-giving love, cannot manifest His invisible self in freedom except through free selves. A person can only express personality through persons, like through like, consciousness through consciousness, intelligence through intelligence. Therefore, The Person must have persons for His free manifestation. Therefore, we are persons.

Immediately there arises the dilemma of all history. If God must have free persons by whom to express Himself in freedom, freedom implies conscious choice, and then free self-expression within the limits of that choice. Freedom is limitless potentiality within the limits of a decisive choice; and we must be sure it is the right choice.

Here we come back on our human level to the same basic choice as we see in the God who is nothing but love and cannot lie. We cannot say that God, the Eternal One, ever made a choice in time, as we do; but we say that God, the Three-in-one, always was love. But for us there is the choice. Having their being in God, created persons could have consciously chosen to affirm that relationship and thus be natural free expressions of the self-giving God. But equally in freedom of choice, created persons can choose to be themselves as if independent of God and live for time and eternity in the illusion, yet dreadful reality for them, of being independent self-loving selves.

While all creation is God revealing Himself on various levels of self-giving love, each according to its divine capacity, we humans as free persons are the summit of His creation. By us, The Person by the persons, He can be fully Himself in unlimited self-giving love, we in our freedom united to Him in His freedom, every limitless human faculty freely expressing Him. He loves and we love, He thinks and we think, He wills and we will, He acts and we act, we humans being in essence God walking about, God talking, God acting, God loving, in John's words, "as He is, so are we in this world".

Are we that? Obviously, derisively, tragically not. Then what has happened? It is not hard to see. Indeed, the Bible makes it quite plain. Freedom can be misused. It can make the wrong choice, which God, the Original Self, never made. What is spoken of as the origin of evil is not difficult to trace.

We have said that a conscious self is only such by reason of the capacity to choose; and every self being an outbirth of the original Self is compounded of love. Every self is love and loves itself. Confronted by the conscious choice of an either-or, it can either love itself by living for itself (in apparent illusory independence in its freedom); or it can love itself by giving itself to union with the divine Spirit of self-giving love.

The Bible tells us what happened. It records the existence of created beings, sometimes called spirits, sometimes angels. Through the misrepresentation of angels in paintings and images, we have a distorted idea of them as half-human with wings, but in fact the Bible calls them spirits; and if God is spirit, and we in our inner center are spirits, then we can recognize others of another dimension who are also spirits.

We are told that their leader, Lucifer, which means light-bearer (which he was destined to be, but not light in himself), did this very thing we are talking about. He chose, not to be the bearer of God the Light, but to be his own light; in other words to find the answer to life in self-reliance, self-seeking, self-magnification, self-satisfaction.

He, therefore, broke open a dimension of the self-life which should never have been exposed, which never was known in God, a dimension where the self expresses itself in self-love, and all that self-centredness produces becomes its way of life—covetousness, lust, vanity, pride, hatred, jealousy, lying and the rest. The Bible speaks of him as a god, for a god is an originator, an author, and this one was the author of this kingdom of lawlessness, which the Bible calls sin. The law of the universe, which is the way the universe works, is God as self-giving love; therefore, lawlessness is every form of self-seeking love.

Here was the origin of a realm of total separation from God, being the opposite to Him, and, therefore, darkness, confusion, disharmony, the slavery of self-gratification, and ultimately for those who voluntarily continue that way what the Bible calls "everlasting destruction from the presence of the Lord and the glory of his power", which in common language we call hell.

Hell on this basis is as rational and necessary as heaven. Yet it can still be said to be "in God": for all self-hood is an extension of His self-hood, and in that sense, as Paul says, "all have their being in God".

But this is a perversion, a misuse of what created selves are destined to be, in union with Him. By refusing that union and its implications, they are still living by God's life in them but it has become negative in its effects in them, producing wrath and condemnation and the death which is separation from Him, and His light in them has become darkness.

Evil is a misuse of self. It is an inevitable potential in a free self, and to that extent is implicit in the existence of selves. A rough illustration is the sun and light. The sun is burning and consuming. If we are in a wrong relationship to it, we are consumed ("God is a consuming fire"). In a right relationship to it, however, we see that the fiery sun goes through a constant process of inner "death and resurrection", by the fusion of its hydrogen atoms, which in becoming helium release the energy which reaches us as beautiful, blessing, gentle, life-giving light, and we live in that light. Yet no fire, no light.

In the same way, a self is a burning fire, whether in God or man. The fire is the source of his energies. In God, His fiery self "dies" to its own independent self-existence, and lives anew in the begetting of His Son and the creation of His universe, and in the Son, the fire is only known as blessed light. We also, as selves out from His self, are consuming fires.

If, in our freedom, we choose just to burn as ourselves and for ourselves, we have diverted the self to a use which never should have been in existence, and which is hell: but if, with our being in God, and now through the redemption in Christ, we choose that He should be His self-giving self in us, then we become light and love in Him.

Here is the origin of evil, and from this we learn

how evil captured our human race; and the record most surely tallies with the facts of our experience. Here are Adam and Eve, the first of our race, capable of intelligent choice, yet not yet knowing the distinction between good and evil. What they do know is that they have a Heavenly Father who has abounded in His love to them in all the good gifts of nature around them in the garden. But He has also conveyed to their consciousness that there is one direction in which they must not go, for if they are to be adult humans, exercising their freedom fixedly in its right dimension, they must discover themselves to be free selves, and made a conscious choice. So they are confronted with a tree of which they must not eat. Implicit in that is an ultimate No to self-pleasing and a Yes to self-giving in God. Here was the crux of the matter. Here was the ultimate choice.

The time came when this god of self-centredness, whom we now call the devil or Satan, presented them with all that could attract them to eat of the forbidden fruit. Humans are meant to be attracted, life is response to stimuli; that is normal, not wrong. But they knew that to yield would be the way of self-pleasing and not their Father's way. By themselves, if they act in independence, they cannot resist, for independent self is self-love and will always go for what it really wants. It is made that way. But deeper than desire is the capacity for choice, the exercise of freedom. It was possible for those two to call on their Father, tell Him of their compulsive desire and that they could not resist it: but to tell Him also that they wanted to do His will, not theirs, and would He rescue them somehow. The means of rescue was there all the time—the tree of life.

All through Christian history the eating of the fruit of the tree has been the symbol of the fact that humanity was created to contain deity, and thus for the union of the human spirit with the divine spirit, for every time we partake of the bread and wine in the Lord's supper, we eat of the fruit of the tree to represent partaking of Christ. If the cry of the heart had been right, the remedy would have been quickly revealed, resulting in the re-direction of the drive of the self-desire. The eating of the fruit of the tree of life would have united the spirit of man with the self-giving Spirit of God, and the light would have swallowed the darkness; for the tree of life, we are told, symbolized the gift of eternal life, and eternal life is Christ. By the same token, the eating of the wrong tree symbolized the union of the human spirit with the god of self-centredness: and it is not difficult to recognize the truth of this Genesis record through all our human history.

That we are a "fallen race" needs no proof when we define the essence of the fall as self-centredness; nor is it difficult to detect the demonic elements in our human behaviour, the one to the other, "man's inhumanity to man" engraved on all the blood-stained records of history, which are only the public records of the private life of all of us.

CHAPTER 4

God Does Nothing by Halves

WHY ARE WE not as we should be? Here is the answer. Which leads to the next question: How can we be what we should be, or can we? The answer is a thankful Yes. There is the way back, as there was the way out. It is rooted in the nature of God. The history of the universe is the love activity of God. Love exists to meet need.

Love is a remarkable word. It is the only word to which debt is linked as a pleasure and privilege. Debts and creditors are usually to be avoided. But love has no other existence than to meet need, and every need has a claim; "Owe no man anything, but owe love one to another". "I am debtor to Greeks, Barbarians, wise, unwise".

Wherever there is need, love has a debt to pay, and need is the creditor. Love *has* to pay. That is why we can love our enemies, because a hurter is in greater need than the hurt. That is why in our rebellion and enmity against God, it is not His hurt that concerns Him, but ours. We are the needy ones, and love exists to meet need. Therefore, we boldly say God had to save. It was not a question of condescension or kindly action, it was a debt of love. God had to save, for love has to save: and we, when saved, have to be saviors.

What did that entail for Him? Something which could be put in quite simple terms. The gospel, the plan of salvation, redemption, whatever name we use, is nothing but God regaining His stolen property. God could not create anything higher than the human race, because God could not create higher than Himself and we are created in His image. We shall receive improved bodies one day, but not improved spirits, for they are in His similitude.

Therefore, the summit of His creation, the human race with all its limitless potentialities, has been stolen, and under stolen management has all its productivity geared to self-seeking instead of self-giving. The gospel is the restoration of humanity to its right ownership, and that is why, when restored, we can, as it were, forget the gospel and get on with living.

Two problems had to be solved in regaining His property. The first was the removal of the consequences of broken law. We use the word law to define the way the thing works, and we say that is the law of its being. It works this way. Conform to it and you will receive the benefits. Defy and disregard it, and you will suffer the consequences. There is a law of gravity. Keep your cup in your hand and you will continue to use it. Defy the law and drop it, and goodbye to your cup.

So with the one law of the universe, the way by which it works, which is God in His self-giving love. Everything which is not the self-giving of God through us humans, but is self-loving self, is broken law. So our total human living, until we are back in union with God, is broken law. The Scriptures leave us in no doubt of the consequences, with such statements as "everlasting destruction from the presence of the Lord": "weeping and gnashing of teeth": "tribulation and anguish, indignation and wrath": "where their worm dieth not and the fire is not quenched".

Plainly then, there can be no restoration of stolen goods to God for the manifestation of His self-giving love until first these consequences coming to all humanity are removed. The way they are removed is the life-line threaded through the whole Bible, and, of course, it is what we should expect —love in action, and love means being other people, taking other people's place. And that is exactly what God did when He took flesh in Jesus and became man and "bore our sins in his own body on the tree", "being made a curse for us", and "suffered for sins, the just for the unjust", and a hundred other such Bible statements. Remove the revelation of the substitutionary sacrifice of "the lamb of God for the sin of the world", and you remove the inner core of the Scriptures from Genesis to Revelation.

If we ask, How did this make the necessary atonement? our simple answer is the statements of the Bible that this was God's own revealed way of redemption, and requires of us "the absurdity of faith", which by-passes reason as merely man's finite analytical faculty, but finds its response in man's centre, in his heart, when he has become honest enough to acknowledge his despair. And yet to reason also what can be more appealing in its perfection—a God who might judge and punish, but instead takes the punishment upon Himself? I have often said, "If you can show me a more wonderful God than that, I will follow Him". I am still waiting!

What did this substitutionary sacrifice do for us? Something more than forgiveness, though that is also included. Forgiveness can still leave behind it the realization that the wrong was committed. But after the sacrifice on Calvary was completed with the cry,

"It is finished", if Jesus had remained in the tomb, there would have been nothing to assure us that it was complete; it was the resurrection that proclaimed that all was settled. And what was settled? "He was raised again for our justification", wrote Paul, because justification, taking us beyond forgiveness, means that the atonement was so complete that we who believe are in God's sight (and our own) as if we had never committed the damnable offenses. They cease to exist in fact or memory, and we are before God and in our own sight as those who had never sinned and are as perfect as He is perfect.

That is a full solution of that first problem. We are like those, as in Bunyan's allegory, who could not get through the gate because of the load on their backs. Our load gone at the cross, we can now enter and proceed on the way. Justification is the gate. The way itself is what matters, and the way is the One Person living His way of life in all naturalness by the persons. Justification is the gateway into unification.

That takes us to the second problem to be solved and the completion of the solution. It was the apostle Paul who specifically clarified the depths of this to us, which he stated in his Galatian letter to be a special revelation. Something more far-reaching is implicit in the fact that when Jesus Christ died and rose again, it was the human race which died and rose again.

The human problem goes deeper than our need of forgiveness, reconciliation to God and deliverance from the consequence of my sin. I am a wrong kind of person and need to be made a right kind. I have an inner core of self-centredness from which I cannot escape. It has been mine from my birth. The Bible traces it to its roots when it says that, instead of being in spontaneous union with the self-giving spirit of God and under His motivation, I have been born in another union; it is a perverted relationship, to that false god of self-centredness, in the illusion of independence, and I spontaneously function under his motivation, without even knowing it.

The Bible speaks of "the spirit that worketh in the children of disobedience", "he that is in the world . . . the spirit of error", "in whom the god of this world hath blinded the minds of them that believe not", "ye are of your father the devil, and the lusts of your father ye will do".

CHAPTER 5

The Other Half

EVEN IF I am forgiven and reconciled, what good would that be if the motivating center of my life remains self-seeking and self-loving? Paul, therefore, and John likewise bring to light a deeper consequence of the fact that when it was Jesus dying and rising, it was humanity dying and rising. If Jesus was humanity on the cross, then, Paul says, He was there as the human race inwardly united to this wrong spirit. Paul spoke of that as Christ being "made sin for us"; and sin is the character of the god of self-love even as righteousness is the character of the God of self-giving, sin is the indwelling spirit of sin which produces the sins, just as holiness is the indwelling Spirit of holiness who produces the deeds of holiness.

Then he says that when Christ (as humanity) died, he "died unto sin". Death is always a separation between body and spirit, so this meant a separation for humanity (represented in Christ) from that false spirit. He lay in the tomb a dead body, and it was the human race there "buried with him". A body only receives life by the entrance of a spirit; so when Christ was raised from the dead, He was "quickened by the Spirit", the self-giving Spirit of God. And we thus rose also, with God's Spirit inwardly joined to us in place of that former false spirit.

Here at last we are presented with the complete

means by which the God of love regains His stolen property. All the meaning of the Christian gospel, all the searchings of all the philosophies and religions of all ages find their answer here. How can man be what he should be? From which would naturally follow the question: How can the world be what it should be? The only answer is: If man could be a person of perfect love, and live the life of perfect love.

But how can he be? How can he escape from the chains of his own self-seeking, which means that he may at best be kind and decent and helpful to the point of preserving his own security; and he may make sacrifices for those he approves of—but not beyond that. He cannot. He cannot in self-centred independent self transcend himself and live vicariously for others; he cannot, as it were, be other people, no matter what happens to him, and he certainly cannot do that for his enemy. That would be a contradiction in terms. Therefore, no philosophy or religion which summons man to self-improvement can give the answer. It cannot reach far enough; and the world can never be set right if I attach any conditions of maintaining my own rights or self-preservation to my self-giving. Somewhere on that route I come to a "so far and no further", and the stream of my love is dammed and the world's problems are not solved.

The only answer is this one: that I recognize that self-centred independence is a perversion, a break-away from the union with the self-giving God for which I was created, and that, therefore, in that condition I can never reach beyond my own self-interest; but I also recognize that God, and He only, the Trinity-in-unity, is love unlimited; and that God through Christ has made a way by which He reunites himself permanently to me. Then in this spontaneous unity, I begin to be this same self-giving love— unlimited: and I am no longer just myself, but I have found the real I in me to be He, and I His means of self expression.

I now need to ask, How can I make this a practical reality? Supposing I have accepted this Bible revelation of God as a fact, and the revealed facts are these: God in Himself is nothing but love: we humans are created in His image so that the true ground of our being is the God who is love: but, in the misuse of our freedom, we have turned our backs on our true being in Him, and have been caught up in the illusion of independence and self-loving selves: God has regained us for Himself by becoming one of us as Jesus the Christ: Jesus, as God in the flesh and representing the human race who have their being in Him, by the predetermined plan of God, accepted a death at our hands.

This death, in our stead, has removed the inevitability of our "death" (everlasting separation from the God of our being), has cleansed away the guilt of our sin-life (continual breakings of the law of love), and has delivered us from "the wrath to come" (the unavoidable effect of our rebellion against the love-law of the universe). Raised from the dead by the glory of the Father, the resurrection was the evidence that all that had to be done in our stead has been done; therefore, we can regard ourselves in God's sight as those who are without sin, justified, righteous in Christ's righteousness.

But also this death, as being we who died on that cross, has cut us off from the spirit of self-centredness, that false god which had immersed humanity in his great delusion, for death is separation of a body from its spirit: and this resurrection, it being we who were buried with Him and raised with Him, was the Spirit of self-giving, the Spirit of love, the God who is that Spirit joining Himself to us, removing the hindrance (the false possessor) to our discovering Him as the God of our being.

CHAPTER 6

That Clever God

B UT NOW I ask myself, How can a general fact become a personal experience? The answer is that simplest of ways by which alone all the generalities of life become personal experiences. It is the simple principle of supply and demand. The Bible calls it the way of faith. We might define it as freedom in action. God has so ordered the universe, all being forms of His self-manifestation, and our relation to it, that we are surrounded, almost overwhelmed, by all that is available to us—food, air, every convenience of life. We have a general recognition and acceptance of the fact that such things are beneficial for us and available to us. We call that believing in things.

But before anything, which is not mine already, can become mine in experience, it is obvious that I must come to want it, and then in my freedom appropriate it. My stomach needs food, it is available and I eat it. My lungs need air and I breathe it. My body needs a chair and I sit on it. But note that the effect of this response of my demand to the supply is that what I take takes me. I take the food and it takes me over for good or ill. I sit in the chair, and the chair holds me, not I it.

So faith, as freedom in action, is only faith when it produces the reflex action. The taker is taken, the grabber grabbed. Faith is not taking, but being taken, not grabbing but being grabbed. And the one and the same principle operates on all levels. There is no secular and spiritual with God. All is basically spiritual for the one Spirit, that One Person, is manifesting Himself through all, and this is the principle of His self-manifestation.

But when it comes to our need of a right relationship to God, we meet a special problem. There is no automatic demand which will appropriate the supply. We humans by no means desire this revolutionary change. We are satisfied with ourselves, or make out to ourselves that we are; we find at least enough attraction in our normal self-interested way of life to be repelled at the thought of any violent change. In fact, we are, as the Bible says, "deceived", "blinded", having been born in the delusion—the product of the Fall—that life is just we living it the way we think best. At most, a little religion, a few good works, satisfy any inner demand for some place in our lives for God and the service of others.

There has to come an awakening, a disillusionment, a sense of need and lack, to bring us to see that we are off the track. The first approach, therefore, that the God of our being has to make to us, to get us within hearing distance of Him, is exposure before remedy. It must be negative before positive: and this approach is what the Bible calls "law".

We have already mentioned that we use the word law to define the only way in which something can properly function. It is the law of its being. Thus we are continually busy seeking and discovering all the laws of our universe. If we attempt to make a thing work against the law of its being, we get trouble. This is true of all the laws of the body, of science, of mathematics, or the man-made laws of social or national life. But there is only one ultimate law, as the Bible has revealed it to us—that God is love. This is what God is. This is how God works. The universe is this law in operation. All is love and compounded of love. This is, therefore, the law of our being, for our being is in God. Anything which is not self-giving love, is broken law, and has its adverse consequences.

We humans instinctively know wrong from right, because, though Adam fell, he did not take the final, absolute step that Lucifer took. Lucifer from the centre of his being rejected God and made himself a god in reverse. To him good became evil, and evil good, self-giving bad, self-loving good. Lucifer became as fixed as a god of self-loving as God is fixed as the God of self-giving. There can be no change in either. There is no response in Lucifer to right ways, no discomfort that he is wrong, he is not savable.

But Adam's sin was not a basic choice of evil for good, not a sin of spirit so much as of flesh. Eve was tricked, and Adam knowingly followed her to keep her, rather than blatantly defied God. When he took of the wrong tree, he chose the way of self-gratification but hoped, as it were, that God was not looking. He hoped for the best of both worlds. Impossible, but it left him with the vivid realization that he had done wrong. He hid himself from God.

Satan does not hide himself. He is in open defiance, he has proclaimed himself as a rival god with a rival kingdom. Adam and we of the human race do not call evil good. We still call good good and evil evil. So we are reachable and savable. Captives of Satan, bound to him, his property, sharing his destiny, but not yet fixed devils. We might be called children of the devil, but not yet sons of the devil. Satan has his being in God but, as a free spirit, has totally rejected even the recognition of that fact. We have our being in God, but, though we are joined to Satan, have not so cut ourselves off by the final choice of our wills and hearts, that we do not recognize or respond to the One in whom we live and have our being.

That is why we humans instinctively know wrong from right: we know that what proceeds from selfishness is wrong, whatever is self-giving is right. Paul truly said that we have the law written in our hearts, and John speaks of "the light that lighteth every man", and the conscience that bears witness to the truth.

But in our freedom, we easily rationalize, we stifle that inner voice and find ways around it. So God, through Moses, defined that law in written terms which we call the Ten Commandments. Jesus defined it in still more absolute and inclusive terms in the two commandments of absolute love towards God and our neighbor.

The normal operation of a law is a perfectly natural functioning of things according to its law—in ease, in spontaneity. So the law by which something works is not normally a burdensome thing or an imposition on it. It is only when it seeks to function against the law of its being, that this law is like an enemy to it. An automobile runs smoothly according to its mechanical laws: pull the wrong lever and it grinds to a halt by being made to oppose its own laws.

So we humans are challenged and opposed by what should be the natural law of our being in God, the life of self-giving love, because we have ground to a halt by the turn of the wrong lever and are seeking to make life work on the unlawful principle of self-loving love. What should be normal, spontaneous, automatic, confronts us in our hearts and by written command-ments as a threatening demand: "Do this and you live. Don't do it and you die."

Law, then, is not God's frown on us; it is the first form of His love. The Bible calls law elementary religion. It is the delicate way in which God reaches us on the only level upon which we could be reached, for love always adapts itself to situations. Being self-satisfied and self-reliant, we would see no point in being told that we need God. Very well then, God meets us where we are in our self-centredness. "You know what you ought to be. You say you can be it. Well, be it. Here is the law. Keep it." How clever and adaptable love is. You aren't conditioned yet for true religion; well, then have a religion on your own level—the law.

We must have the wrong way exposed to us which in our blindness we try to make out is the right, before we are conditioned to desire or find the right.

CHAPTER 7

The Answer Begun

THE EFFECT OF this inner and outer law on us is two-fold. On our response hangs our eternal destiny. We can either respond by hyprocisy or honesty. As a fact, we all start by being hypocrites. That is, we pretend to ourselves and others that we keep the law reasonably well, enough to salve our consciences: We have enough religion or a philosophy of some kind to cover our tracks, for a self must always have a foothold for its selfhood—a righteousness (rightness) of some sort. What we really do is to try to keep the eleventh commandment, to hide the truth from ourselves as from others—"Thou shalt not be found out!"

Honesty is when by some means or other (God has a thousand original ways), we are brought up sharp enough in our lives, suddenly or gradually, to be faced with the plain recognition that we are not what we should be. We are law breakers. The moment of truth is when in our freedom we admit that fact. That is honesty, and that is also a total self-humiliation. The supposed foundations to our selfhood have given way. That is why there is a cost in it. The false front of our self-justifying religion or philosophy collapses.

But this admission of merely being a law-breaker in the sense of not living up to the standards of God's law is not sufficient by itself. The point is that it is the law of *God*, and, therefore, the law on which our being is founded, so that we are at variance with the Source, the Originator, the Upholder of our being. Therefore, we are at variance with life itself. We are wrong, we are lost, we are in the dimension of what Jesus called "outer darkness".

Now when that is an admitted reality to me, I am conditioned for the truth. I have a need and I must have it met. I can no longer consciously continue at variance with the God of my being and under His justifiable condemnation, with its necessary ultimate ending in "everlasting destruction from the presence of the Lord". What then shall I do to make amends? But that is exactly what I cannot do as a self-confessed law-breaker with the usual consequences of law-breaking.

This is the moment, the first moment when He who is love, the ground of my being, can get over to me what love is and what He is, and what I am to be. Jesus Christ, God in the flesh, is the answer. What He did for me and as me was what I could not do for myself. This is the eternal love. Now in my total need I am conditioned simply to see with thankfulness that what I could not do to remove guilt, condemnation, ever-lasting separation, He did for me; and they are no more. Seeing is recognizing and receiving and release.

In my freedom of choice, which hardly was conscious choice, when my need was so desperate and the supply so complete, I suddenly realize that God is now my God and Father, and Jesus Christ my Savior and Lord; and not only have I a conscious peace and release, but I have a love for Him. What I probably do not realize is that this is the beginning of my living the eternal quality of life for which I was originally created. The restoration to God of His stolen property has taken place. A revolutionary change has taken place. For the first time in my human history, I love someone else more than myself. A new love, greater than my love for myself, has taken possession of me: love for God and Jesus.

I do not yet realize that this is not my human affections. I probably think this is my love for Him, but what has really happened is that in receiving Christ I have received into myself the One who is love, and what I regard as my love for Him is really the first expression of God's self-giving love in me, loving another more than myself, "The love of God (not love for God) shed abroad in our hearts by the Holy Spirit". This new love, greater than love for myself, has taken possession of me, causing me to start being an other-lover: for I very soon find that if I have love for Jesus, I also have love for all men, for He and His world are identified. I find in myself, not only the love for Him, but also the desire that my friends, my neighbors, and all men should share the secret of life that I have found and that they equally need, and that I should take my share in the ministry to mankind in all ways available to me.

This is eternal life which is eternal self-giving love begun in me. I have "come home", and begun to be the light and the love I was destined to be. What we call Christianity, therefore, is not belief in a doctrine, not membership in a church, not allegiance to a Bible or a Jesus of history, but a new love; for again we say, we live where we love, and this new love is for the first time in my human history the love of someone more than myself: and this is and means a new quality of life of which the potential and implications are way out of sight beyond space and time, just as an Amazon river starts by a trickle at its source, or a prairie fire begins with a spark.

CHAPTER 8

The Answer Continued

HOWEVER, THIS HAS not completed the exposure to us of our mistaken concepts of life, as though it is we living it. We are so used to this illusory outlook that, though we have now recognized and admitted that we did not live our lives on God's standards, and in our lost condition needed and found a Savior, we now think that, as Christians, we can set to work and live on a new level. We will seek to keep the commandments, to love God and others, to maintain communion with Him by prayer and Bible reading, to conquer the habits that defeat us, our hates and fears and lusts and jealousies, to have God at the center of our domestic, business and social life, to attract others to our new-found faith.

Instead, what happens? We begin to find this new life wearisome. We have not what it takes to live it, neither sufficient love for God and our neighbor, nor sustained interest in prayer or the Bible, nor victory over our weaknesses.

We even lose the consciousness of God's presence. We cannot handle our depressions, our failures, our relationship problems, the strains and stresses of modern life, the difficulties of even attempting to be honest and pure and not self-seeking in the jungle warfare of modern industrial, political, and even social and domestic life. To say that we approach a conformity to the absolute demands of loving God with all our heart and mind and our neighbor as ourselves, is ridiculous, and frankly we often do not want to. Maybe we had better give up. Maybe life was easier and more enjoyable without trying to be a Christian in a serious sense. We seem nearer to a breakdown and the need of psychiatric help than to the peace and rest and adequacy we thought the Christian life had for us.

Good; all these are excellent signs. In our former unredeemed life, we had to be so disturbed that we came to a final crack-up and admitted our failure before God, a total failure. Despair is the best word, for despair means that we are finished and there is nothing more we can do about it. We have to come there, having given up completely, before we can have eyes to see that when we could not climb up to Him, He had climbed down to us; what we could not do for ourselves, He had done for us.

Now, again we have to come to a second despair. Before, our recognition was that we had not done what we should have done in keeping God's law. This time, as redeemed Christians, we come to the discovery that we cannot do what we should do. Before, we learned our guilt. This time, we learn our helplessness. Before we did not, now we cannot.

The apostle Paul has a profound and subtle explanation of this stage in our experience. He has already shown how the law (God is love) should have been naturally operative in us, so that we are love; but owing to our fall into self-centredness, that same law then confronted us with its demands which self-love cannot fulfil, and thus at last led us to honest admission of our lawlessness.

He goes on to show, mainly in his Romans and

Galatians letters, that because we are still not yet free from an innate self-reliance, from the idea that somehow as new men in Christ we can do what we didn't do before, once again the law confronts us with its "You ought", "You must"; and in our illusory self-confidence we jump at the bait. "All right, we will," we say. "We'll do the best we can." And down we fall on our faces. We don't fulfil it, and usually we don't even want to fulfil it. We prefer to please ourselves.

Often the preachers from the pulpits are themselves to blame in their constant exhortations to us to get up and get doing what we can't, and don't honestly want to—for the simple reason that independent self, self-relying self, can only by its very nature be self-pleasing self. So we come to an impasse. The law, according to Paul, is now completing its job on us. It forces us to face, first our guilt, but now our helplessness.

The Bible is full of illustrations of sincere men, earnestly dedicated lives, who went through the period of their disillusionment, when they had to discover that they could not be or do what they wanted to do. Outstanding are the disciples of Jesus, who were completely sincere in saying they would die for Him, but they ran when the heat was on, Peter to the point of denying Him with curses; and that was just where they learned this second and final lesson—their inability.

I learned it, to give a word of personal experience, when I was as dedicated as I knew how to be. I had responded to the call of God to take Christ to the Congo. That cost me nothing, because I could conceive of no higher honor than to introduce Africans to Him to whom I had had a personal introduction through an Englishman. When out there, my aim was single and concentration total on my calling. But I carried with me this illusory concept we are all born with—that I was a servant of Christ and wanted to be the best I could be; and yet I was terribly conscious that I was not what I should be. Particularly, I had not the kind of love which would identify me with those to whom I had gone, or the faith that the things would happen I had come out to see, or the power to see them happen: and when I am dissatisfied with my standards of ministry, I take it out on my wife by irritability, and my fellow-workers by criticism which must not admit that they have what I have not.

So, though active without, tramping the villages to speak of Jesus, up in the early morning for a couple of hours with God and the Scriptures, within I was unhappy. I began to think that I had been happier before I gave my life to Christ than after. I was bound by self-consciousness, inner strain, disturbed relationships.

I was passing through what I since learned is a stage we all have to pass through when we are miserable Christians and, as I did, think we were happier in the old life than in the new! Sometimes it has been called "the dark night of the soul", "the wilderness experience", "the dry and thirsty land where no water is", with much more self-consciousness than God-consciousness, more self-concern than concern for the needs of those for whom I had come to Congo.

But, unknown to me, my real trouble lay in another direction. I had the illusory idea that I needed to become something better than I was: I must be a better representative of Jesus Christ, and so forth. I was looking for personal improvement and some further spiritual equipment which would set me on my feet. God and the Spirit were then to be my helpers.

I sought God and searched the Scriptures, as any

earnest Christian would do. Surely there in the Bible the answer was to be found, for it talked of love and faith and power and freedom. But the answer I got was in very different terms. It was a confrontation, not this time with the law saying to me, "You ought", but with God turning my attention from myself to Himself by saying to me, "I am". The way it came to me was in that statement I have so often quoted, "God is love". But the emphasis was on the little word "is". It struck me that I had been seeking a God who would say to me, "I have and will give to you." But instead, He was merely saying, "I am", and not "I have". It was as if He were saying to me, "You've got it wrong. You thought love was something I had and could therefore share with you. But love is not a thing at all. I *am* love."

Then I saw that the only self-giving love in the universe is a Person, not a thing. Therefore, it is not something He could share with me, but it is Himself, and He can't take parts of Himself and give to me. He can only be Himself. It was my first sight of an exclusive God, the One Person in the universe, who gives nothing but is everything, and, therefore, His only giving is to give Himself and just be Himself wherever He does give Himself.

How then do I have my needs supplied, if God has nothing to give me, but in each instance I find that He is (not has) the power, He is (not has) the life; until finally I read that "Christ is (not has) all, and in all"? That last phrase gave me my key. I saw that my mistake was the idea that He would give me things, and that I would thus become something. Now I saw that we humans do not exist to become something, but to *contain Someone*. This was a totally different concept, and was the end of my great human illusion that I must be this or become that, centering my attention on what I am or ought to be, and equally depressing me with the recognition of my failing to be all this.

Now I saw that I am to cease to look for improvements in myself, or to center my attention around what I feel or don't feel, whether I am this or have that, why I fail in this or am defeated by that—the whole outlook on life which fixes my attention on myself and my reactions or my adequacies or inadequacies.

The most illuminating illustration I found in the Bible was the several times we are called vessels, because a vessel, a cup, a vase, a can, is strictly limited to one function only. It only exists to be a container. It can be nothing else: and here was this simple though humbling illustration of my relation as a human to God. I only exist to contain Him. A vessel does not become the liquid it holds; they are separate, unmixable entities: so I as a human do not become the power or love or wisdom of God; I merely contain Him who is all these, and everything. How clearly I saw that: we humans are not created to become something, but to contain Someone—but that someone is the living God, and, therefore, the All.

This transferred my attention from worrying about myself as the vessel not being this, or being that. Leave myself alone. I am just the container. In place of this, I had it clearly that I was containing a totally exclusive Person who gives nothing, but is all; and I don't contain Him in a relationship in which He imparts various gifts and graces to me, but I am just a means by which He can be Himself in a human container. This means that my main function in life

changes from activity to receptivity. Activity centers
round how I can be this or do that, around my human
self. Receptivity is occupied with receiving or recognizing what I contain—the only function of a vessel.

I saw how all life is in this same relationship to God.
Vegetation exists by what it receives—sunlight and
rain. What it receives it utilizes, but it must receive
first, then activity is a by-product of receptivity. All
science is application, not creation. Scientists discover
what is, and then apply it. We humans have lost our
way because we are blinded to the fact of being containers of God, and have substituted our self activity.
We have to return to the roots: and it is not even really
receptivity, but recognition, for having already received Him, we form the continuous habit of recognizing
that we do contain Him. Life at its base becomes a
repetition of recognition. What more amazing realization can there be than that we humans contain God?

This is why Jesus stated that rest is the evidence of a
life in gear. He said to us His followers, "Take my
yoke upon you . . . and you will find rest unto your
souls; for my yoke is easy and my burden light." An
obvious contradiction in terms. Life is activity—the
yoke is pulling the plow: but how can a plow be easy
to pull or a burden light to carry? The answer is the
difference between activity from inadequacy which is
strain, and activity from adequacy which is rest. If we
are pulling the plow of our life's problems, relying on
our own resources, that is strain, for we haven't got
what it takes to meet them. If, in our pressures, we
turn inwardly as containers to Him who is the all
within, and boldly reckon on Him to handle things,
then it is rest in the midst of the activities—the habit
of recognition.

CHAPTER 9

The Answer Completed

WE HAVE NOW found that the key to life is, not assistance or partnership, but replacement. Redemption from our sins was not something half and half. It was not we being able to do something for ourselves in getting right with God, and then He helping us out. It was only when we saw we were lost and done for that we found, not assistance, but replacement. His blood for our sins. Now we find that there is no half-way house for ourselves. It is not He helping us to live, and we in partnership with Him: it is He replacing us. His blood in place of our sins, His self in place of ourselves.

We can never stress this too much, because all the burdens, distresses and problems of us Christians have their source in our old, old habit of looking for some ability or enablement in ourselves, and often the exhortations from the pulpit give the same misleading emphasis—you *ought* to love more, pray more, be better, etc., then feeling desperate because it isn't there: whereas the truth is that, as old tin cans, we don't look for change or resources in ourselves. This is the point—humanity does not change, but we move over in our inner consciousness to Him whom we contain, who doesn't change us but is the Changeless All within, and Him we affirm as all we need.

What we have to learn and experience about ourselves and the relationship of humanity to Deity is now completed. They were absolute lessons—the lessons of replacement. They could not be learned without exposure before remedy, and it had to be absolute exposure. There could be no shred of recognition of His blood in place of our sins, or His self in place of ourselves until we had come to the total end of our self-justification, and our own self-reliance; usually these two lessons are learned in succession, the one before we are redeemed, and the other after; and each entails a total brokenness, conditioning us to recognize and accept the total replacement.

With this relationship in clear focus, it is safe for us now to turn around and pay attention to our humanity, and give it back its rightful place. It has been a case of the disappearance of the human self as a background for its reappearance where it really belongs. We never were, of course, pots but persons. But we had first to know, and know for ever our pot relationship—that it is the exclusive He and never we, and we not becoming something but containing Someone. When we have so learned this that we shall never depart from it, but know we are vessels for ever, we the creature, He the Creator, neither one ever becoming the other, nor mixing in that sense, then we are free for the right form of self-affirmation and the total uninhibited activities of the liberated self.

Our discovery, then, is that our actual relationship with God is not that of vessels containing Him, but of a unity, Person with person, which could not be possible between two inanimate entities, such as a vessel and what it contains. Indeed, in this sense, the vessel analogy, if regarded as a complete illustration, is misleading, because it can leave us with the mistaken impression that our relationship with God is variable, just as a cup may contain liquid at one moment and be emptied at another; whereas the real truth is an indivisible union, in which there can be no such thing as sometimes a fullness, sometimes emptiness, or a partial filling. When we feel like that or believe it, we are accepting an illusion.

The point is that the actual fact of the relationship of the union cannot be safely realized, or lived by, until once and for all it has sunk into and become fixed in our consciousness that He is always the all, and we nothing but the container, the vessel. That is why the vessel relationship is a necessity as a permanency in our consciousness, before the union relationship can safely be to us what it really is.

The analogies of the union given by Jesus and Paul are likening our relationship to Vine and branch, Head and body. In each case they form a unity. When we look at a tree, we do not divide in our minds between trunk and branches, we see one tree—a unity. Equally a head and body form a unity, and we regard them as such. When we see people, we do not see so many heads and bodies: We see just persons— a unity. We do not even speak of a union, which directs the attention to two coming together to make one. We speak of a unity where the two have become one. So it is with the Trinity and us.

Now we come to what we have already seen to be God's sole purpose in Christ dying and rising, and we with Him: the destruction in death of the old union with "the spirit that worketh in the children of disobedience", and the union in resurrection with "the Spirit that raised up Jesus from the dead"—God Himself: and the union has produced the unity. This has been the fact in all of us since in our need and in our freedom, we saw, believed, and received the Christ of God. From that moment (whether specific or dateless) the unity was a fact. He had joined Himself to me and I was joined to Him. As Paul said, "He that is joined to the Lord is one spirit." In that unity, He has become the real I, again as Paul wrote, "I live, yet not I, but Christ liveth in me."

In other words Paul did not say that he and Christ lived side by side within him, as if it was, "I live *and* Christ lives in me": but that though he was a living human, as much after conversion as before, yet the real Paul was no longer himself, but another Self in his place: "I live yet not I, but Christ lives in me." The real Paul was Christ walking about and talking, just as Paul wrote in another place, "Ye are the temples of the living God; as God hath said, I will dwell in them and walk in them."

That is why Jesus had said, "Ye *are* the light of the world," not "You *have* the light." If we have a thing, it is not we, but just something we hold in our hands, as it were. But Jesus did not say, "You are darkness, but you have me who am light." He said, "You *are* light." But how could that be when we are darkness and He is the light? Unity. Because He and we are one, therefore, he says, "You are the light." That is why John wrote, "If we love one another, it is God dwelling in us and his love perfected in us." Our loving is really He loving by us. Again unity.

CHAPTER 10

How Does Theory Become Experience?

I NOW NEED to ask myself again: How can a general fact become a personal experience? Even if I mentally accept the fact of union with God, how does that help, unless I know it in my inner being? How can I be among those of whom it was said, "They were all filled with the Holy Spirit" or as the prophet of old said, "I am full of power by the Spirit of the Lord"? The answer is that simplest of ways by which alone all that is available in life becomes personal in our experience, and although we have already stated this, it is important enough for repetition and close examination. The Bible calls it the way of faith. We might define it as freedom in action. God has so ordered the universe and our relationship to it, that we are surrounded by all that is available to us—food, air, every convenience of life. We have a general recognition and acceptance of the fact that such things are there for us. We call that believing in things.

Belief is mental acceptance. We believe in thousands of things as realities, but that belief does not produce in us a personal experience of them. Experience is a product of a deeper level. That comes from the center of our personality, our human spirits, our ego, where knowledge and desire combine to motivate acts of will. That is freedom in action. That is faith in contrast to belief. Something is available—take the simplest—

food, air, a chair: my belief takes me that far. But if I am to choose something, I must desire it. So to availability is added desirability; and we humans are so made that we are a continual stream of desires, for we are made of love.

Now when a thing is available and desirable, is it reliable? At that spot we have to stop short. Nothing in the universe can be proved by reason and observation to be reliable. Reason can take us up to the edge. It can make things appear the nearest thing to a certainty; but it cannot prove things as a certainty. No one can prove that the food I eat will agree with me, or the chair I sit on will hold me, or the house I buy will suit me.

What do I do then? A thing is available, it is desirable, it is reliable so far as I can estimate. That is as far as I can get. So now comes the moment—the moment of faith, the moment of freedom in action. I have to leap into the unknown. I have to go beyond reason. From the center of my personality, called in the Bible my spirit or my heart, I have to make a deliberate choice, a leap into the dark.

That is exactly what puts movement and adventure to living. We have to gather together all the certainty we can about a thing, but in the end we have to move out from uncertainty. We are always the gamblers, putting our money on what seems to us the nearest to a "cert".

So life is no smooth flow from certainty to certainty, which would be stagnation to the human personality; it is an unending series of leaps, the choices of faith in action. Down to the tiniest and most trivial of actions, everything is an inner choice of faith, freedom in action.

But those leaps, and they alone, give birth to personal experience. All the chairs in a room may look nice, be available, and look secure. They are meaningless to me beyond the general fact of my believing in them, except for the one I sit in. That involves my inner choice and outer action. I desire a chair, I think it is reliable, but without final certainty— I sit. Then I have personal experience. I cannot then say that chair would hold you, but I can say it holds me, and makes me feel it holds me. I have taken it: it has taken me. So with eating food, so with breathing air, so with every human action up to the great decisions of life. Only such personal action produces experience, and brings something down from an available generality to an individual reality. But it does always do that. What we link ourselves to, links itself to us, and makes us know it.

It is true that higher attainments of faith may take a little longer to settle themselves in us. We learn a trade or a language. It is an act of faith: the language is there, we involve ourselves in starting to learn it: that is faith. But we go through a long period in which we have to walk by faith, the endurance of faith, taking hold of something which seems constantly to elude us, sounds which seem to go in one ear and out of the other; we by no means at once are taken hold of by the language. But the time comes, perhaps with us hardly realizing what is happening, when what we sought to take has taken hold of us; the language, the trade, has become spontaneously part of us. Faith, persistent faith, has produced substance. It is no longer the general fact of this trade, this language; but *my* trade, *my* language.

Now we come back to the question we first asked.

God and I a unity by grace: spirit joined to Spirit. How does this generalization based on the Scripture revelation become *my* experience? By this same method. In place of a belief in this as a fact for humanity through Christ, I take personal action—inner action. Available? Yes. Desirable? Yes. I have come to the point where nothing will be more wonderful and desirable, and nothing more hopeless than struggling along in the old illusion of separation. Reliable? Well, the God and Father of our Lord Jesus Christ as revealed in the Scriptures is the God to whom my heart wholly responds and before whom my reason prostrates itself as the highest conceivable: I am, therefore, ready for the leap.

From the center of my being, with my will, as being my heart's desire, my choice, I affirm Him and myself to be in the eternal relationship He says we are, through my crucifixion and resurrection with Jesus Christ: we are a unity, He in me, I in Him. I state that as a fact. It has nothing to do with what I feel about it or with my sense of unworthiness and inconstancy, and the unreliability of my humanity. He planned it. He effected it. He chose me, not I Him. Very well then, though I may think He makes queer choices—facts are facts.

The inner choices of the will are given outward expression in the body, as when we choose to sit in a chair, we then sit. So the inner action of the will in this greatest of all affirmations is confirmed by confession of the mouth. Some opportunity is taken to express our faith-in-action to ourselves and to others: I did it with my pen, drawing a picture of a tombstone with my name on it which I could visit to remind me of the end of an old union to a false god. It took a little time longer to have an equal consciousness of the resurrection!

But the all-important consummation of such faith is that what we attach ourselves to by the act of faith attaches itself to us, and makes us know it. Food in the stomach, air in the lungs, the chair we sit on, have all become conscious realities to us. So in the ultimate dimension of faith—the realm of the spirit.

By our act of faith we are identifying ourselves with the Christ whose atoning sacrifice reconciled us to God: and there settles into our inner consciousness an awareness that we are forgiven, accepted, justified in His sight as if we had never sinned, adopted into His family. It produces a peace, a solid certainty of a new relationship, something inwardly substantial in our spirits. It is God the Spirit, to whom we have attached ourselves, bearing witness with our spirit. Faith has produced a substantial awareness of Him in whom we have placed our faith in action, and of what He has done for us.

So now, this highest dimension of faith, not merely in our reconciliation to God, but in His eternal, unchangeable, factual unity with us, equally produces its settled awareness of this supreme fact of human history. It may not be in a day, just as spontaneous familiarity with a trade we are learning does not become ours in a day. But it comes.

Sometimes it is with electrifying suddenness. The gift of tongues was the evidence to Christ's first followers at Pentecost. That same gift has been in operation in many in these recent days, and by that they know inwardly with never a further question that they and God are one.

To others, the inner awareness comes in different

ways—to me not till after two years from my committal of faith, and then by a kind of flooding of inner certainty—that was all.

But the point is that faith has not completed its function until it is consummated by an experienced certainty of the thing appropriated. Until then, whenever concerned about it, keep repeating the affirmation of faith in much the same way as a learner keeps repeating his lesson, until the subject matter has become part of him.

CHAPTER 11

At Last—The Spontaneous You

THE WHOLE POINT of what we have been talking about is that man—we—should be what we should be. We said at the beginning that that was the point of the Bible. It is written about man: man's origin: man's fall: man's restoration: man's activities: man's destiny.

We all say that the problem of our world is the problem of us who live in it. Now we can begin to see what man is and how he can be what he should be. We have seen that man is truly man when he is an inner unity—in such a relationship that the Real Self in him is God, yet he is also a truly human self: the Bible description is He in us and we in Him. But because it is a unity, we as humans are restored to our normal functioning as humans. The emphasis is removed from God and on to us. We have had to spend pages talking about man's disappearance, getting our false concepts of self out of the way to make room for the True Self. But when we have that fact in true and established focus, and for ever in our settled inner consciousness that the one who really lives our lives is He, and not we, then we can turn right round and restore our humanity to its right place. Having disappeared, we reappear! And we reappear with a bang!

Man is really man, we are really we, in the total

liberation of all our human potential: and a human potential no words can compass. All that we distinctly know that life should be—purpose, adventure, usefulness, gaiety, seriousness, harmony, ultimate meaning—every faculty of mind and body "tasked to its highest", limitless in outreach—all is ours. Jesus said no idle word when in the darkest moments of His few short years He said, "I say these things to you that my *joy* might remain with you and your *joy* might be full", and joy is an apt way of putting in one word all that life at its fullest should mean to us.

The time has now come to affirm our humanity as well as to affirm His deity, to accept and appreciate ourselves as well as Him. The unity makes this possible, because the unity produces a spontaneity. We can now live our lives, taking for granted the adequacy which is He, the other part of us. Life cannot be lived on any level by duty or effort. Life is just living, that is all.

On the physical level we are in a spontaneous relationship with our bodies. We don't have to wake up in the morning and try to remember the five laws by which the eye sees before we start seeing, or the ear hears before we start hearing! All is automatic, spontaneous. That is what makes the delight and ease and zest of living: we see, we hear, we speak, we act without a moment's consideration of how those members of our body function. The proof that we must have spontaneous bodies is that, the moment a member gives us trouble, we visit the doctor. We must have the spontaneity restored.

But the true spontaneity of life is not physical, but spiritual: it is the given relationship of unity with God, with Christ, with the Spirit. That is why we have spent

TO THE READER

It is a regrettable fact that in stressing the exalted power and transcendence of God the evangelical church today has tended to neglect the corresponding truth of our Lord's immanence. Sensing this lack, Mr. Grubb in certain of his writings has emphasized the opposite extreme, feeling that this is needful. And it is.

However, in making his points, it is unfortunate that Mr. Grubb has not always been as careful as one might desire with his terminology; in fact, he has sometimes found himself hampered by certain weaknesses of the English language itself—and the result is that some of his expressions sound quite similar to what a pantheist might use. We recognize and deplore this flaw. However, in the very same writings Mr. Grubb makes numerous doctrinal statements with which no consistent pantheist could *possibly* agree. This fact fully supports Mr. Grubb's clear declaration that he is *not* a pantheist. We feel that the mature reader will recognize this readily.

Mr. Grubb tends to begin his doctrinal books with sweeping summary statements, and for some readers this has caused problems. It is as if he assumes that the reader has already read his earlier books and knows what he means. If such is not the case with you, we trust that you will withhold your judgment until you have read the elucidations which follow in later chapters.

We trust that as you digest this challenging book you will experience the deep blessing to which so many others testify.

Sincerely,

THE PUBLISHER

so much time, and the Bible gives so much space, to getting an exact understanding of this unity by grace, and of it becoming our spontaneous experience.

Now we can live as humans, yet really we know, and never for one moment of time cease to know, that the hidden life is God in us, the subterranean stream, the subconscious Self: "our life is hid with Christ in God . . . Christ is our life." (Col. 3:3,4). But now, because of the spontaneity, we can get about the business of life, and there is a sense in which we forget God in our daily occupations, on the level of our external activities which are meant to occupy our full attention and demand all we can give them.

This is not wrong. It is normal and right. It is not forgetfulness; it is in fact God and I doing things together, but with the external emphasis on me, as if it was just I doing them. But I know better! I don't, however, condemn myself at the end of a busy day because I have not had time for many conscious thoughts of God. If I should come to God and say, "Forgive me for not thinking more of you today", He would answer, "You weren't meant to". You don't spend time during a day asking yourself whether you are really there, do you? God is your other you, so you don't need to keep asking whether He is there either. You and He are one. What you are doing, He is doing; you are doing it together.

We have, in fact, to pass through three phases in our attitude towards and understanding of ourselves. We start life by a false attempt at self-appreciation. We try to make out we are all right: "going about to establish our own righteousness", the Bible calls it. That finishes when we become honest about ourselves in the sight of God, and our repentance toward God and faith toward our Lord Jesus Christ is an end to our false self-appreciation.

This is followed by often a long period of self-depreciation. As new-born Christians, we are making the discovery that it is not in redeemed self, any more than it was in unredeemed self, to be what we should be. So we are much more conscious of our failings, our inadequate human selves, than we are of Christ in us. We condemn ourselves, we stress our weaknesses, we speak of our hunger and need, our inadequate love for God, our sins. We say that if God does anything with our lives, it is in spite of us (whereas in fact it is because of us), and so forth. This is the phase of temporary self-depreciation, necessary for us to learn the truth about ourselves, but only temporary. As we have said, it is spoken of in the Bible as the "wilderness experience".

The third and final phase is rightful self-appreciation. From false self-appreciation, through temporary self-depreciation, to true self-appreciation. This is when in the unity we have found for ever we are only the vessels that contain God; but we are vessels, and more, we are vessels who are really persons; and our humanity is now the self-expression of the Living God. *We* are the light of the world. We are the eternal love in action. The center of our inner consciousness has moved over from self-depreciation to God-appreciation and thus to self-appreciation. It is a significant proof that we have not life yet in gear, we have not yet come full circle, when our normal reactions in situations are to emphasize our weakness and need rather than our ability.

"I can do all things," said Paul. "We are more than conquerors," said Paul again. "We are well able to overcome it," said Caleb. "I am full of power," said Micah. But in each case they added that it was "through Christ", or "by the Spirit of the Lord", or some such statement. However, the primary emphasis was not on Him in them, but on themselves, and they "able ministers of the new covenant"—through Him. Their emphasis was not on their weakness but on their strength—by Him. This is the true self-affirmation.

CHAPTER 12

Just Be Yourself

THIS IS A matter of great importance because nothing dogs our footsteps more in our Christian living than our constant sense of condemnation. We are such failures, we are such weaklings, we are so up and down, we are so cowardly, we are so fruitless, and so on, and so on. It continually shows itself in the easy way in which we downgrade ourselves as useless, more a hindrance to God than a help, so rebellious, so disobedient, and as we said before, so fond of saying that if God uses us at all, it is in spite of us, not because of us. Our troubles are not really the things we do or don't do, but that dragging feeling that anyhow we are no use, and make such a mess of things, and look at how God uses so and so, but not me. Or it is merely the heavy feeling: we don't feel bright, we don't feel loving, we don't feel spiritual; but we do feel out of touch, dull, dry, tongue-tied.

This is why to understand how to accept ourselves as well as Himself is so vital. Let us get it straight again. The major point is that it is He who accepts us, and He who chose us. If it depended on our choosing Him, we might continually hold back, for how could we know He would accept such as us? But He chose us—unconditionally. "Ye have not chosen me, but I have chosen you." He chooses us exactly as we are, with every facet of our humanity. We may well laugh at the strangeness of His choices, but that is no business of ours. We had better get busy choosing ourselves, if He has chosen us. To accept Him and not accept those He accepts is to insult Him.

In fact, we need a thorough springcleaning of our condemning, smearing, guilty ideas we so often have inherited or picked up somehow about our human natures. That is why we think that the wide openness of today, though it shocks many because of its abuses, is actually much healthier and much nearer the truth than the hush-hush of past generations. And no book can be more baldly open than the Bible. No spades are called shovels there.

Let it sink into us that there is not a single reaction that we can have as humans, not a single response of our bodies, minds, emotions, imaginations, which is intrinsically wrong. Let us drag such things to the surface and, instead of condemning the instincts or reactions, examine how misuse can be replaced by right use. The negative is to say that a thing is wrong, conceal it if you can. The positive is to face it and see how God's purpose is to use that very tendency as some channel for His outgoing goodness.

We always regard the word repentance as referring to some wrong things to be admitted, confessed, and put away. But it merely means "change of mind". It can, therefore, also have a positive direction; it can mean that, instead of only shame and humiliation for various human tendencies and habits, we begin to dare to accept that they can be part of the armory of God in our human make-up for manifesting Him and ministering to others.

The foundation to such a positive attitude must be, first, that we recognize a rightful title to the full

acceptance of ourselves. We can do that when we have
seen that our human nature has not been and is not
the source of either good or evil. We have continually
said that we have the human race in focus when we
see that we have always been the containers of a god.
"Greater is he that is in you than he that is in the
world," as John wrote, "and hereby we know the
Spirit of truth and the spirit of error." And Paul in
Romans, that we all are slaves to a master and owner,
whether the sin spirit or the Holy Spirit.

As a consequence, in union with Christ we recognize
every good thing as solely He in us: "The fruit of the
Spirit is love, joy, peace . . ."; "Jesus Christ is made
unto us wisdom, righteousness, sanctification. . . . "
Equally in the former union with the devil, every evil
thing was the fruit of the evil spirit: "Ye are of your
father the devil and the lusts of your father ye will
do": "He that committeth sin is of the devil . . . for
this purpose the Son of God was manifested, that he
might destroy the works of the devil."

Redemption, therefore, has released us humans
from our former task-master, and joined us to our new
Lord. The old man has become the new man. The
same man (human) in both relationships, but the
change of an old lord for a new one. In the light of
this, we can accept ourselves, with no single thing
about our human nature which is not now for God-
manifestation: and wherein we still have difficulty
with aspects of our humanity, it is not for us to despise
or smear ourselves, but to inquire how these same
aspects can now be harnessed for new uses.

Let us also remember that that Accuser of the
Brethren is a born, compulsive liar; therefore, one
favorite weapon of his is to make us appear in our eyes

a distorted, disgusting caricature of what we are in others' eyes. Sufficient for us always to return to the fact that God has chosen us exactly as we are, and if He is satisfied to do that, we can be satisfied; and He has far more pleasure than sorrow over His children. Read Numbers 21:23. And when we hear that the judgment seat of Christ will be something to be feared with deprivations to be expected, I prefer to believe what Paul said in I Cor. 4:5—that every man shall then have, not rebuke and punishment, but "praise of God".

So replace the waves of condemnation with boldness of faith. Long ago I learned that "the voice of the stranger" depresses, downgrades, darkens; that "the voice of the Shepherd" is always gentle, upbuilding, healing. Discern between soul and spirit* where the soul, the seat of the emotions and reason is variable and can convey variable impressions to us, as much lowering as elevating; but we live back beneath the outer covering of soul, where our spirit is joined to His Spirit, and there the relationship is invariable, and there He is in all his sufficiency, no matter how the outer storms may blow, or we may "feel" a poor recommendation of Him.

That we do deviate on occasions can be understood when we remember that slaves, though slaves, always retain their fundamental freedom. Look at it this way (and we understand our present relationships as slaves to a master when we read the word in Romans 6:16 and following verses as it is in the original, not servants, but slaves).

Our humanity was the captive of the god of self-centredness, "the spirit of error". We were his slaves,

* See Chapter 16 of *God Unlimited*.

and as slaves we were his property and did his work and obeyed his orders. But even a slave is still free by nature. Therefore, as all men have their being in God, we knew what we should be and expressed our freedom in a limited way by having some religion and doing some good works; but we were still slaves and our life was identified with our Master's and our destiny was His. It was like a slave in an old Roman household, who did his master's job all day, but at nights when his master was carousing, he would express his own indestructible freedom by slipping out and doing what he wanted.

But now, by giving ourselves in our freedom to our new Master, who had conquered the old one in His death and resurrection, we have freely become His slaves, do His work, and are identified with Him. Because we are for ever free, we can and do listen at times to the enticing voice of the old master and do some of the things we used to do and should not: we express our freedom downward, even as in the old relationship we expressed it upward. But slaves are slaves and back we come in shame and confession to find forgiveness and to continue our life with our new Lord.

That is how unredeemed men do good things while still remaining unredeemed, and redeemed men do bad things, though remaining redeemed. But note that just as an unredeemed man cannot continually live the new life because the wrong seed is in him, as John wrote: so equally the redeemed man cannot live the old life, he "cannot continually commit sin", because "he is born of God and his seed remaineth in him".

In our freedom we have found the law of our being

in God and made our fixed choice in attaching ourselves to Him: our freedom now expresses all its
potential within the limits of its new alignment, but
being always free in this mixed world of good and
evil, we can and do temporarily respond to outward
enticements to the old, wrong way; but they do not
reach our center, where as slaves to God, He holds us
fast and pulls us back to where we belong.

This is Paul's teaching: in Romans 6 where we have
freely exchanged the old slavery for the new: in
Romans 8 where we live in the liberation of the new
life: and back at times to Romans 7 where we forget
our new relationship in Christ and are enticed back
into some of self-indulgence; and there we find the law
awaiting us with its perennial challenge to independent
self, "Thou shalt not", and back in our illusory
independent self, we are condemned and guilty, but
helpless to resist our self-love, for self cannot expel self,
until we see our foolishness and return to where we
belong.

So now as liberated humans, as true humans with
all our human potential, as purified humans (the word
"pure" means unmixed, and the Bible speaks of our
having pure hearts, pure minds and pure souls,
because we were unmixedly slaves to the god of this
world—though in our freedom occasionally doing
good things; and now we are unmixedly slaves to
Christ—though in our freedom occasionally doing bad
things), as such, we live our normal human lives, and
our living is God living.

In other words, Christianity is not a religion or
denomination. It is not people gathering for worship
in special places at special times. It is not a doctrine or
theology or ritual. It is people being ordinary people,

and that is God living in human flesh. We re-discover a secular God in the home, the store, the office, on the roads and at the desk. We divest God of particular types of clothing, a special religious language, just as much as we know He is not limited to male or female, color or class. God is to be found as a common person in common people. No one was commoner than Jesus, nothing particular about Him.

"Is not this the carpenter?" they asked. "There is no beauty that we should desire him," said the prophet. Yet those who had anointed eyes said, "We behold his glory as of the only begotten Son of God, full of grace and truth." So God is seen in common men. That is the height which humanity scales.

We live our normal lives. That is the will and plan of God. We *are* the will of God, not we find it. Our acceptance of ourselves starts there. That means accepting our background, our upbringing, our years maybe of the life of a prodigal, wounds we may feel we received in an unhappy or broken home, in lack of education, in physical disability, in unjust dealing, in wrongs committed against us. Paul said it when he wrote: "When it pleased God who separated me from my mother's womb and called me by his grace, to reveal his Son in me." He did not say that God's hand started to be on him on the road to Damascus, but at his birth and through all the years of his self-righteousness, culminating in his leadership in the persecution of the Church. So we boldly say that, as part of an eternal destiny, all that has happened to us, have been ways of God's moulding of us. Now we are what we are and that is God's planting.

So we live, relaxed in the sense of not questioning who we are or what we are, but being ourselves—

housewife, business or professional man, white collar or blue collar worker, student or executive. All we are we put into our vocation—energy, application, creativity, team work.

We are not afraid of using our minds and wills on the daily decisions of our lives. There are times when we can lift up our hearts in a flash of faith or inquiry; there are multitudes of occasions when we just decide and act, taking it as fact that "we have the mind of Christ", and acting on the given basis of the unity. We live as fully emancipated human beings, which we are, running our own affairs: we ourselves know and are conscious of a kind of envelopment of light within, the inner subconscious presence like the flowing of an underground stream.

This is the "I yet not I" life, in its simplicity, singleness, liberating self-activity. This is man in action, which is God in action.

CHAPTER 13

If It's Tough, Good!

O F COURSE, LIFE is no smooth flow. If the Bible says it is from faith to faith, and from grace to grace, we can add it is also from problem to problem!

What do problems or pressures do to us? Or temptations? They consciously involve us in situations. We cannot float quietly along past rocks which make rapids. We are aroused. We have to do something about them. Aroused humanity is exactly where God can express Himself as God. In the multitudinous situations of the world around us in which we have no particpation, we can make no contribution. They do not affect us, and we do not affect them. But where we are personally involved, there we have an effect, and God by us.

Our human pressures and involvements, therefore, are the one and only way by which God through humanity can reach humanity. It is the principle of the incarnation, and the reason why it is God's predestined plan that we should be fully humans in every kind of human situation. Jesus was "tempted in all points as we are". This gives full meaning and intelligent incentive to our acceptance of James' word, "Count it all joy when you meet various trials". They have a vital purpose, every one of them.

But just at this point there is something we need

clearly to recognize about our humanity. We humans are the negative to God's positive. No positive can be manifested except by contrast with and absorption of its negative. Each is necessary to the other and belongs to the other as its polar opposite. You cannot know light except in contrast to dark, or soft except in contrast to hard, or yes without no. Light is invisible unless it is reflected against a non-light body, such as the moon or earth, and swallows it up. Then you don't see the moon but the glory of the light, or the earth except as clothed with all the colors of the light. A soft bed must have a hard framework, but the mattress must conquer the bedstead! Flesh must have bones, a decisive yes derives its strength from a conquest of the alternative no's. So we are God's polar opposite. We are the "are-nots" in relation to God's "I am".

Paul speaks of us having "this treasure in earthen vessels that the excellency of the power may be of God and not of us". He so clearly saw this fact and principle, when he told how he had a thorn in the flesh which God did not remove though he besought Him three times. Instead God said, "My grace is sufficient for thee: for my strength is made perfect in weakness": and Paul added that, therefore, he took actual pleasure in unpleasant situations, "infirmities, necessities, distresses, persecutions", because "when I am weak then am I strong".

In other words, all our awkward situations and our normal negative reactions to them—dislike, fear, unwillingness, inadequacy, frustration—are the only way we can react as humans. If that is all we are—just humans—then we would be in bad shape, enchained in the prison of our own reactions. But to us who are

at home in the fact of the Other Self—the not I, but
Christ in me—pressures, trials, temptations are a
springboard to faith. We dislike a person, so we take a
leap of faith. We move over and say, "I don't like this
person, but You are love in me. You love him, so with
Your love, I love him." Switch on the light, and where
is the darkness? So with every kind of negative reaction.

But note, it is not we who are changed. We do not
look at ourselves and expect to see a change in ourselves. No, we affirm Him and go forward: the effect
on ourselves is not the point. We fear. We affirm His
courage in us and go forward. We have doubts. We
say, "God is my God. That is settled for me." We have
not got what it takes. We say, "God is my strength",
and do the job. We resent or object to a situation. We
say, "God's ways are perfect. I accept and praise."

The point is that our negative human reactions are
necessary to God. The positive must have its negative
for its manifestation. We do not, therefore, blame or
condemn ourselves because we are the have-nots, and
guiltily feel we are wrong to react as we do. We are
what we are, and what we are meant to be. We may
well laugh at ourselves, but not throw ourselves out
with disgust. We are not God's liabilities, we are
God's assets.

The secret is always replacement. We don't work
hard at pushing darkness out of a room. We turn our
backs on the darkness and switch on the light—where
is the darkness? We transfer our attention from the
negative to the positive. That is the secret. Not
resistance, but replacement.

Let us have it clear: our humanity is for the manifestation of Deity. For this to be possible, we humans

are to be involved in the whole of human existence. Personal involvement in any situation generates personal reactions. I participate, I feel, I react. I am now an aroused human in that situation. But my responses are negative. I have not the courage, the ability, the love, the wisdom, the answers. I am disturbed by frustrations, opposing personalities, wrong-doing, misfortune. This is exactly as it should be. Now I am a conditioned human—conditioned for the leaps of faith. What I am not, God is: and God is not at a distance, we are joined—one spirit. He is my Other Self.

So I move over in my inner center from my personal reactions to affirming Him, recognizing Him for what He is for every situation; and then I go forward right in the situation, just the same human in myself to all appearances, but actually it is God on the scene, God working, God manifested, God glorified.

CHAPTER 14

Quick Down, Quick Up

HOWEVER, I DO not always leap upwards in faith under my pressures. I sometimes jump down. That is when I sin. My human reactions, though negative, are not sin. They become sin when I follow them through negatively: my dislike for a person, instead of being replaced by God's love, continues unchecked as hate: I fear, and, instead of exchanging fear for faith, I take flight and run away from God's will: a feeling of impatience or resentment is expressed in the angry word or lost temper, instead of being swallowed up by God's patience or quiet acceptance of His way. Anger is right when expressing genuine concern for others: it is wrong when, as so often, it is to compensate my own hurt feelings. Pride is expressed in magnifying Christ ("making my boast in the Lord", as the Bible calls it) or it can be in making much of myself.

Though even at this spot we have to beware of the bondage of false condemnation. We are real selves as well as it being Christ in us: therefore, we do have pleasure as well as giving Him pleasure: we do have motives as well as being motivated by Him. If a person thanks me because something I have said has made Christ more real to him, I have no necessity every time to stop him short and say, "Give the thanks to God." In thanking me, he really means as a channel,

and I as a channel am rightly also pleased that I have
been a channel for Him. I must not accuse myself of
pride because I do feel pleased.

Equally, when my main motive in some action has
been believing it to be God's will, yet I discern also
that I had a personal motive of the gain or enjoyment
I also get from it, I must not therefore condemn
myself. As a real self, I have my pleasure, my motives,
my sense of personal gain in a thing. The point is that
that is not my main motive. God's will, God's work,
and God's glory is my main objective; as it is He by
me, I too anticipate pleasure, satisfaction and gain
from it.

This is how it is with God Himself. Years ago I
began to justify my conscious egoism by discovering
that the Bible said of God that "for thy pleasure they
are and were created", and of Jesus Christ that "for
the joy set before Him He endured the cross". "Then
God does things for selfish reasons", I said, "the same
as I do." Of course, I had missed the point which I saw
later, when my own self-centredness had been exchanged for God-centredness. I saw that true living
is when the purpose is for others, and the secondary
effect is the pleasure or gain I have from it. False
living is when my pleasure or gain is primary and the
purposes of my living incidental. This is true in all
life's activities, such as the simple difference between
eating to live (and incidentally getting pleasure out of
it), and living to eat!

God's pleasure, Christ's joy are an outcome of His
giving Himself, not pleasing Himself. True pleasure is
when my self-pleasing is fulfilled in self-giving, and my
self-love finds full satisfaction in other-love. There
is total self-fulfilment. Self exists to be fulfilled, whether

God's self or ours. There is self-sufficiency and a consciousness that we can be what we should be and do what we should do. But, as Jesus said, we find ourselves by losing ourselves in God's love activities, and the reflex effect of such living is the pleasure, gain and satisfaction it brings us. Paul said it: "As dying and behold we live": "As poor yet making many rich": and yet finally returning its rich treasures on us who, though having nothing, yet find we possess all things.

God's everlasting joy "and the good pleasure" He finds in His will, and all the outpoured adoration seen by John around the throne in the Book of the Revelation is the response to Him, Father, Son and Spirit, of a creation which has its being in His self-giving love, and a redemption which was Himself in His precious blood going to final limits in redeeming His enemies by dying for them.

We, the redeemed, though we do not live a life of continued sinning, do commit sins, usually sudden and unpremeditated. What then do we do? We have not broken relationship with God, but have interrupted fellowship from our side of the relationship. We have asserted our freedom by acting as if we were not one with Him; but were once again our independent selves and going our own way. Just because we are one with Him, we are guilty and know it.

The way back is as simple and plain as on our first coming to God. If there is quick sinning, there is quick cleansing. It has to start at the point of my personal freedom, where I went wrong, and I must express that freedom in honest confession. That is all I can do about it, but that I must do, and that means my brokenness. It may involve confession to man or restitution, but it certainly means admission to God of my sin. When I do that, it is as if God says to me, "Yes, you sinned, and honest confession and repentance were necessary. But as for the sin, I settled the whole sin question 2,000 years ago in the atoning death of my Son. Through him sins are no more. I have forgotten them. You can forget them."

At this point we have to be careful not to add a second sin to the first. The first was the sin itself, the second and greater is if I don't believe at once that what God has cleansed, He has cleansed. Not to believe in the efficacy of the blood of Christ is a worse sin than the first, for unbelief, Jesus said, is the only real sin (John 16:9).

Some are also troubled by the repetition of sins in their lives. How can they be delivered from doing it again and again? The answer is that Christian living is not in the past or the future, but only in the present. The Bible word is "walk", continually used in the New Testament. Walk is present tense and can only be a step at a time; and the walk is with a Person, with Jesus. Therefore we do not find deliverance by looking to the past or future for some fool-proof formula; but forgetting our search for deliverance, we become occupied by the simple walk with the Deliverer. Put it this way, as some African Christians said: "Leave the past under the blood, leave the future with God, and get walking!" Live in the present. Again—if we sin, take the way of repentance and get cleansed. Don't sin what the Africans call the second sin, which is not believing the immediate efficacy of the precious blood, for unbelief is the worst sin of all. Praise and thank, whatever one may feel, for praise is the verbal demonstration of faith.

Don't then be concerned about constant repetitions of the same sin. Deliverance from repeated acts of sin is not to be had by looking at the sin or at myself, and wondering how repetition can be avoided; it is by the daring look to Jesus, and the leaving of the problem of repetition to Him. The past is no longer there through Christ, the future is not my business; so if at this moment you are walking with Jesus, be thankful. If and when the sudden fall comes, get in the clear again with God, and walk on—looking neither to past nor future. Walking with Him is the way ("I am the way"), and we are much less likely to be tripped up in such a simple single-eyed walk than if we are tense about the past or future and holding on to some supposed formula of deliverance.

Even if we are bound by a habit, or even if we are not willing to be delivered from a habit, the deliverance or the change of will to make us willing can never come by our attention being centered on the habit; but only again by a daring leap of faith which affirms that God is our deliverer and that He is the one who makes us "will and do after His good pleasure", therefore we take it by faith that this has happened here and now, though we feel no difference, and we boldly walk out on the settled fact.

Sin, indeed, is not the real problem, but the guilt that follows, which condemns and binds us. This, again we say, is Satan's secret weapon. He will trip us up by some subtle temptation. Having got us down, his real purpose is to keep us down by the pouring on of condemnation. We must, therefore, know how, when tripped, to get up quickly, to get standing again in the armour of God and keep walking. Faith is the means. Faith which is action, and by which we boldly thank

God that the sin is no more. We may go on feeling guilty or stained, but we turn our attention away from the feelings and we replace them by faith. We replace guilt by praise, and walk on with Him as before.

CHAPTER 15

You Are an Adult. Be One

WE COME TO the ultimate question when we now
ask what, anyhow, is the meaning of life? Why
do we live it? If unclear here, we are unclear every-
where. We had better know and know with an absolute
certainty: and there is an absolute certainty.

The Bible subdivides this life into three distinct
stages, and presents these stages in great distinctness
and by several different methods of presentation. The
fact of greatest importance is that we recognize that
two of the stages have been left behind by us, and are
past history, and that the whole of our life is now lived
in the third stage.

We might compare the first two stages to the
foundation of a building which must be strong and
fixed; but when we are sure of that, we leave the
foundation alone, forget about it, and live in the
superstructure—equivalent to the third stage. This is
of such importance, and a definiteness and finalty of
having left the first two stages and come to live in the
third so absolute, like the crossing of a great gulf, that
we will note the several Bible statements, which under-
line this fact. They are found in Paul's letters to the
Romans, Ephesians and Philippians: in his letter to
the Hebrews: and in John's first letter.

The clearest and simplest to start with is John's,
because he uses the human analogy of birth and

growth. But we should take a warning here, because
biological growth is reckoned by our time factor—so
many years for each stage. Spiritual growth, however,
is not of this dimension, not bound to our human
timetables, but is a product of faith. So soon as a
person sees and appropriates his right to be in any or
all of these three stages, he is there! If spiritual growth
is regarded as gradual as in a biological sense, it can be
used as an escape mechanism for not being more
advanced: "I have not grown to that stage yet." That
would be a growth by works—but growth is by faith.
Believe, affirm, appropriate—and you are there! That
is how young converts often leap clean over the heads
of us older ones.

So John uses the three stages of little children, young
men, and fathers (I John 2:12-14). The first two, he
says, are equivalent to infancy and adolescence: "I
write unto you, little children . . . young men." Both
are growing-up stages which are for the convenience
and benefit of the child and youngster. The child, he
says, in I John 2:12-14, knows God in the primary
relationship of a forgiven sinner being received into
the family by the Father. It is an external relationship.

Then the adolescent begins to find that he has a life
to live by his own resources and not just by his parents.
He has to move on from total dependence on his
parents outside him to finding the inner strengths
needed for adequate living. So the Christian adolescent
has to find the secret of inner adequacy. Now it is to be
Christ in him, as well as coming to the Father through
Christ. It is an internal relationship.

Then the big leap is between adolescence and
adulthood. Graduation for an adolescent means
technically the end of his training days when all the

concentration has been upon his personal development. Now he leaves himself behind as a recipient and becomes a contributor. This is the big leap. All that was involved in the training years goes into the subconscious, as it were. It becomes the hidden and almost forgotten foundation upon which the living superstructure is built.

So there is a sense in which we leave behind the lessons of our training days in the Spirit. There is the sense in which we forget the Gospel, forget Christianity as the ladder by which we climbed to adulthood. Unity is graduation. Unity means that all that had to become fact in us through Christ, had become fact—"joined to the Lord one spirit". Therefore, that which led up to the graduation ceremony can always be looked back upon with interest and thankfulness and, of course, shared with others in their stages of need, but not to be looked upon again as something which has to be repeated in our own lives.

So adulthood is the great leap, the training days are over, and now life is on the productive level. Concerning Christian adults, John uses a curious phrase that the fathers (the reproducers) "know him that is from the beginning". We pass from God external to God internal, to God universal. This is no longer God for our personal benefit, but we joined to Him as partners with Him in His purposes from eternity to eternity. He is no longer even given the personal name of "Father" or "God". He is The Universal One, "him that is from the beginning".

This three-fold delineation is equally clear in Paul's massive and most comprehensive outline of the redeemed life—in his Romans letter. First, justification (Chapters 1–5). Then, unification (6–8). Then the redeemed as a co-redeemer in all of life's relationships (9–16): towards our own countrymen (9–11): in all the activities of the daily life, business, household and local church (12): in politics (13): in questions of using our mature liberty as a ministry and not a stumbling block to other believers (14): in missionary responsibility (15).

In his Ephesians letter, Paul takes us through crucifixion and resurrection to the life of the ascension. Crucifixion and resurrection were the completion of our personal deliverance. Then from the throne, the ascended Christ, "far above" all His enemies whom He has conquered, now returns to earth again in His Spirit to gather the spoils of His conquest. And we are His Spirit-endued agents. Having been crucified and risen with Him for our own renewal, we now share the throne with Him in the sense of exercising the authority of faith over all His and our conquered enemies, and we go out from the throne in His Spirit to lead the devil's captives back as His captives, as we were led back ourselves. This summit life, the third form, the savior-hood life is presented here by Paul as the product of faith, "according to the exceeding greatness of his power to us who believe" just as personal crucifixion and resurrection are experienced by faith in the Romans letter.

In the Hebrews letter there is a tragedy. It is Christ as our Moses redeeming us from the world: Christ as our Joshua taking us into promised land where we enter into His rest through ceasing from our own works: and Christ as our Melchisedek, our eternal high priest.

But the writer stops short when he begins to speak of Melchisedek (Chapter 5). He is writing to a redeemed people, "holy brethren, partakers of the heavenly calling", but though redeemed, their hurt human selves under the pressure of their afflictions were blocking their vision. They were stopping short at adolescence. Christ for them, yes: Christ in them, yes: but Christ by them for others, no: they were too occupied with their own human hurts.

Christ as Melchisedek is the high priest of whom it is said that He is "taken from among men, and ordained for men in things pertaining to God" (5.1). In other words a priest is one who is redeemed from among humanity, then a commissioned person to return to humanity, to relate them to the God to whom He has become related by grace. The high priest expresses his priesthood by us, who are called by Peter, "a royal priesthood"; but this fact is not mentioned in the Hebrews letter, because the writer says that they have become dull of hearing. When they should have become teachers of others (a priesthood ministry), they had need of being retaught themselves. Instead of contributors, they could only be recipients, instead of adults, adolescents.

So without actually saying that we as priests on earth bring to man the eternal, spiritual benefactions of the great high priest—the covenant of the eternal union (8), the continued present cleansing (9), the privilege of being ceaseless self-givers (10)—he states these as the benefits bestowed by this "unchangeable priesthood". He only implies, for those who have eyes to see, that the priests bringing the eternal benefits of the high priest to the human race have been constantly among us, these men and women who by faith (11) were the agents of God's redeeming grace, each in their generation by all variety of means.

Paul finally puts these three stages of our relationship

with God into the words of his own personal experience in perhaps the richest and profoundest outline of the spiritual pilgrimage ever written in a few short sentences, in his Philippians letter (3:7-11).

In place of the vanity of his self-righteousness, he has now found Christ's righteousness (v. 7). This was infancy. To know Christ excelling all else as his indwelling Lord so captured him that from henceforth it was to be all for all. This was adolescence (v. 8). At first the transference was painful, he "*suffered* the loss of all things". Then a change began. What once seemed costly to lose now became offensive to think of maintaining. A great reversal, and the change was from interest in a Christ who was a benefit to him, to interest in a Christ to whom he should be a benefit, or at least a sharer of and collaborator in His interests.

That he might "win Christ" became his ambition. To win a person is to gain an entrance into his inner heart where he can freely share his most intimate interests with you. Christ's interests are the redemption of the world, so Paul moves with Christ from being redeemed to being a co-redeemer. He secures himself *en route* by stating (v. 9) that this is not to be sought or gained by his own self-effort, but is as much and only at the disposal of appropriating faith as were all his former benefits through Christ. But this now meant for him, in the power of a personal resurrection by which the Spirit of self-giving was joined to him, that he shared with Him the vicarious sufferings unto death as a co-savior, which would result in a resurrection not merely of his own body, but, as with Jesus, bringing many sons unto glory.

It was the same in the life of Jesus on earth. His infancy and adolescence were completed when the

Holy Spirit came on Him at His baptism and drove Him into the wilderness to settle it once for all, under the fires of temptation, that He was not for self but for God. He had "graduated". From that moment onward, everything that happened to Him was in no case for His benefit, for His maturing, for His testing. It was all in every detail something for others. There was no other meaning to every incident, without exception. And so with us. Now in our adult life not one incident, not one situation, is related to something for our benefit or trial or enlargement; it is wholly for God's saving purposes by us in others.

CHAPTER 16

The Great Why and the Total Answer

NOW, HAVING SEEN the three stages, and the fact that, first reconciled and then united to God through Christ, we have passed into the third stage, we again ask: What does that mean?

We are living: God and we are living. Why? Obviously the question to be answered is: Why does God live and therefore we in Him?

Do we not return to where we began? To the one simple statement—God is love. And love means that other people's needs are more to us than our own. Life then, if it is love, is living other people's lives as our own. We saw that, in the revelation of God as the Three-in-one, in the begetting of His Son, God is reproducing Himself in love. The eternal love-stream is flowing, and the Spirit is the stream in the universe.

We saw how the creation bears its own witness to the kind of person God is by the fact that it silently, though involuntarily, gives itself for us. The true life of the corn of wheat is not in the cornfield; it lives again in us. So with the rivers, truly flowing in our bodies as in all living things. So with the trees which furnish our homes, and so with the whole earth, filled with its glories and beauties, its treasures and substances, whose destiny is fulfilled in serving us.

Christ gave Himself for us, and God was in Christ reconciling the world unto Himself. John said that this was the essence of love. It meant and means that love cannot be hurt with what hurts it. It only knows one hurt, and that is the hurt of the hurter. It is not the killed who is hurt, it is the killer whose deed kills himself. So God who is love has only one hurt through history in the fall of the human race. Not the hurts we have inflicted on Him by our hates and sin and rebellion; but the hurts we inflict on ourselves, the eternal destiny of the damned. That has hurt God because He is love, and so hurt Him that He must save us.

Our need is His concern; so Jesus came to meet our need and take our hurt on Himself. He called Himself bread, meaning that His real living would be by becoming our life. God really lives by living the life of others: Jesus as bread, Jesus as living water, Jesus as the light of the world, Jesus as the door of the sheepfold, Jesus as the good shepherd—all mean the same thing: that the person who is love finds the meaning of life in being identified with others, in meeting their need, in taking their place, in being them.

Did not Jesus on Calvary so become us that it is said that when He was crucified, we were crucified, buried when He was buried, and risen when He arose? Is He not now our life? "Christ lives in us", "Christ who is our life". "In all our afflictions he was afflicted". "I was an hungered and ye gave me meat: I was thirsty and ye gave me drink: I was a stranger and ye took me in . . . Lord, when saw we thee an hungered and fed thee? Or thirsty and gave thee drink? . . . Inasmuch as ye have done it unto the least of these my brethren, ye have done it unto me". The identification is so complete that He is saying that hungry, thirsty, naked man is He.

That is how far love goes, and God is love. It goes to the limit. It is a new interpretation of the meaning of life. We humans give our lives, maybe, for those we approve. God's love has no reservations: it is total, unconditional. So Paul said: "Peradventure for a good man, some would dare to die. But God commendeth his love toward us in that while we were yet sinners, Christ died for us . . . when we were enemies, we were reconciled to God by the death of his Son." Christ gives His life for those He disapproves; for below their hate and guilt and rebellion, indeed, because of it, He knows their dire need; and God lives to meet need and gives Himself without limit to do it. That is a different quality of love, and only God is this kind of love. What is God's joy? What is His pleasure? How does He complete Himself or express Himself (for, as we have said, a self must have self-completion and self-expression)? What is life, this eternal life, in its ultimate meaning?

The answer is given us in the God who has shown us exactly what He is in Jesus. It is in self-transcendence. God's life is others having life: God is blessed when man is blessed; God sorrows when man sorrows: God (in Christ) moves into man's earthly hell when man is in hell, to get him out of it: Christ lives His life in man, so that man in his turn now, through God in him, begins to live other people's lives. The gaiety of God, the seriousness of God, the joy of God, the sorrows of God, the song, the laughter, the eternal livingness of life, the total meaningfulness of eternal life—here it is.

And then John quietly writes: "For as he is, so are we in this world". Not "ought to be", or "could be", but "are." Of course we are, this new life is He in us. So we are now the eternal love. Exactly what He is, we are. That is the end of our self-preserving selves! God unlimited is love. Man unlimited is love. If we forget we are only the negative in ourselves, we quickly say, "Absurd. Impossible. We are self-lovers." But we are not, for the real we is not we, but He. "Love your neighbor as being yourself" is the command. If that command comes to us in our independent selves, it is hopeless. But it is to set the absolute inescapable standard, the *sine qua non*, of a new kind of man—God in a man, and man thus able to do this and doing it. We must do it, we do do it, because we can do it— through Christ.

Paul did it. "To the Jew I became as a Jew . . . to them that are without law, as without law . . . I am made all things to all men that by all means I might save some." "Now we live if you stand fast in the Lord", he wrote to the converts.

Moses was so identified with the people of Israel as he led them through the wilderness that when he pleaded with God over their sin with the golden calf, he said, "If thou wilt forgive their sin—and if not, blot me, I pray thee, out of thy book which thou hast written." He was they. What happened to them, must happen to him. He loved them as being himself.

Stephen did it when bleeding and dying under the stoning of the Jews. His face was "as it had been the face of an angel", but his heart was with his persecutors, not with himself in his dying agonies, not even with Jesus whom he saw standing at the right hand of God. Their need was where he was—in their hate and blindness, and his last prayer was, "Lord, lay not this sin to their charge."

Without doubt that was what pierced Paul, equally blind but honest, and quick to recognize another quality of love which his religious faith did not give him (for his religion was really only the religion of all natural men, projected self-love, *his* God), and if Stephen loved like that, Stephen's Christ and God must be like that: and Stephen gave us the apostle Paul.

CHAPTER 17

Applied to the Daily Life

IF, THEN, I am as He is, how does it work out in practical life? It means a revolution in my outlook. Normally, I interpret all happenings of life in terms of their effect on myself. My physical condition, my home affairs, my business affairs, my social life—how do they affect me? What difference does this situation, this crisis, this tragedy or problem, this success, make to me? If I am a Christian, I may seek a Christian interpretation—this is for the testing of my faith, for the maturing of my walk with God: but still it is in terms of its effect on me. But we have already said that the way things affect God is the opposite: not their effect on Him, but on us. Jesus living our lives. So now with us.

The new outlook is: This has happened to me as some way by which I am to meet the need of others. As Paul says in that Second Letter to the Corinthians, in which he most fully shows what living other people's lives means: "All things are for your sakes."

The fact is, and the change which has taken place in us is that it is no longer a question of either my own life being for myself, or of God being for my convenience, or my salvation, or sustenance.

So I practise a changed outlook. My normal human reaction will always be: Why has this happened to me? But now I say: This is for others. I move over within from my outlook to God's. I may not in the least see how it is for others. It may be merely that my going through a tough experience with God fits me to share and show the way to others going through the same without God. Paul said he was comforted in all kinds of afflictions, so that he could share the secret of that same comfort with others in like afflictions.

The point is the habit of always relating all things that happen to me to the meeting of some needs in others. It is the difference between frustration and opportunity. If I just see things as happening to me and I don't know why, I am frustrated. I say, "If only things were different, if I hadn't had that difficult past or this physical disability or family problem, I could be of some use", then I am bogged down. But if I say, "God, you have sent this for some purpose, to minister somehow through me to some people in need", then it is opportunity. Life is then always an adventure of faith, never dull, never repetitious, always with some meaning round the corner. Let us get it in its total dimension—life's only meaning is God and others.

It helps us also to get it clear that everything that comes to us comes from God—what we call evil as well as the good. God, of course, is not the cause of evil, but deliberately directs everything for good ends. The Bible uses strong terms of "God sending" the unpleasant as well as the pleasant, and sending is a positive word, not just a passive permission (for many talk of the "permissive will" of God).

Peter in his first speech after Pentecost said that they had taken and crucified Jesus "through the determinate counsel and foreknowledge of God". No mistaking that. God determined that wicked men should do what they purposed to do and it would really fulfil His purpose—

which was to save the people doing it! Such is God!

Joseph said that by his brethren selling him into slavery, God "sent me before you to preserve life . . . you thought evil against me, but God meant it unto good".

Whatever happens, we say, "All right, God, You sent this. It may tear me apart to say so, but I say so." From there the next step is easier, "God, this has some purpose outside of me to meet the need of others. Just show me what."

The important fact to recognize is that God has only one aim in His present dealings with our world—to get all of us who will respond to Him off the wrong road on to the right. It was said of Jesus "that the world through him might be saved". It is a matter of eternal seriousness, for it concerns eternal destiny. It has to be through man to man. A savior must be where the people are who need to be saved. To save a drowning man, you get in the water beside him. So God became man to be the Savior.

To bring the given salvation to all people, God still has men. They are the saved who then become saviors; not, of course, saviors in the sense of the one Savior Jesus Christ who completed our salvation, but in the sense in which the Spirit of God is still doing His saving work by Christ's spiritual body, which is we, as He did by His physical. In that sense we are co-saviors, co-redeemers. Indeed, Moses was bold and said he was going up Mount Sinai to "make an atonement" before God for the people, which he did. That means, then, that every situation we are in, God puts us in, and it has some saving purpose in it.

CHAPTER 18

Life in the New Dimension

PRIEST IS THE Bible title for this ultimate category
of life, and intercession the work of the priest. We
understand, of course, that, in Bible terms, priesthood is not some specialized "sanctified" office, but the
inescapable ordained condition of every redeemed
person. Redemption is at the same moment ordination
into the priesthood. All members of the body of Christ,
without distinction or discrimination, are, according to
Peter the spokesman of the apostolate, not only a
"chosen generation", but a "royal priesthood". Since
the old Israel failed to rise to its privileged commission
of being a "kingdom of priests" (Ex. 19:6), the new
Israel has received the appointment. God's priests are
very ordinary people, and very secular people, for
they are you and I.

We need, then, to be clear about what the office of
priesthood involves, and the work of intercessors,
since we are these. We have already stated it in the
general terms of Hebrews 5:1. The priest has been
"taken from among men" (redeemed); "ordained for
men" (commissioned): "in things pertaining to
God" (to bring men to Christ and build them up in
Him).

Get that down to specifics in our daily lives, and we
see it best if we understand what is meant by our being
intercessors—the chief work of a priest.

In the Bible an intercessor is anyone, everyone, who sees a situation with God's eyes and moves in on it. That is to say, the whole of our life, all our lives, are full of frustrating, yet challenging situations. God, it said, "wondered that there was no intercessor" and "looked for a man to stand in the gap and make up the hedge".

Millions of gaps, millions of hedges, some in every one of our lives. But the point is to have eyes to see them, and we are exactly positioned, everyone of us, appointed from before the foundation of the world, to be just where we are and what we are—to fill some gap, make up some hedge.

So every life is nothing but a mass of opportunities, and we have been put there to seize them and grasp them. Intercessors, therefore, are not some peculiar people, any more than priests are, but are you and I, in the most ordinary business, workshop, domestic situations; put there because there is something, it may be in our own households, in our church, district, city, country, world, which we are meant to have eyes to see as intercessors, and to stand in that gap.

How do we see, then? First, by having scales of self removed. Being humans, and meant to be humans, as we have said before, we always start by disliking uncomfortable situations, and being hurt by them, resenting them, or being bored by them, questioning why such things should be in our lives; or maybe nominally accepting them as what we miscall the cross, and putting up with them: or, if they disturb our routine and challenge us to sacrificial action, finding some reason to leave others to handle them. This is not wrong. It is right. It means that we are humanly involved and thus livingly related to a situation, and can, therefore, be a vital factor in it. No involvement, not within range of response.

But while we remain hurt or resistant, we cannot see beyond our hurt selves. The way is blocked.

Look at Hannah, the mother of Samuel, hurt because God did not answer her prayer by giving her children, while the other wife Peninnah, though godless, had them. Taunted by Peninnah, which made the hurt worse, she had one refuge from her frustrated self: at least she was her husband's favorite to whom he gave special gifts at the great event of the year, the visit to Shiloh. Year by year she lamented God's unkindness to her and had what the record called "a fretting faith". Better that, however, than no faith like Peninnah! Because when we are God's, even the frustrating years are really a build up of pressure for the moment of revelation.

But that moment has to start by a death to our self-outlook to make room for God's; and God knows how to take us to our grave (when we are His and can "take" it). One year, Hannah's hidey-hole for her self-comfort was gone! Her husband, Elkanah, turned on her. He was tired of her fretting, miserable praying and tears. "Hannah, why weepest thou? Why eatest thou not? Why is thy heart grieved? Am not I better to thee than ten sons?" A nice humble remark for any good husband to make!

Her last refuge was gone. She was out in the cold by herself, or she would have been if, like Peninnah, in her moment of crisis she had had only herself. That is where a crisis becomes a desperation without God. But Hannah knew God, and the moment had come when He could speak a hidden word to her, and she could take it. Did she not realize how selfish all her praying had been? She wanted sons just to prove that God was with her, and maybe to have an answer for Peninnah. Why not change the thing round and want a son for God's purposes, not hers? She saw the point and struck a bargain of faith with Him. If He would give her a son, He should have him, even if she never saw him again.

We know the sequel: the birth of Samuel, one of the great men of history. Later she had four sons and four daughters of her own—perhaps more than she bargained for! But little had she known or seen till that crisis moment that this was putting a great purpose of God's grace through a travailing intercessor.

An excellent illustration of how the most ordinary of domestic situations is a platform for a great exploit of faith. We see the point. *Every* situation always starts with a resistant human self. It must do, because that provides the necessary foundation of an involved self. Now the first step forward in being God's intercessor is being taken. It is a step down, not up. It is a death experience. The hurt self has to be recognized for what it is, not wrong, but the first evidence that God is looking for His intercessor in a situation, and that we are that man, for we are involved in it.

But when frankly recognized, we accept our privilege as a privilege, not as an imposition on us, and we see glory in the cross. For this is what Paul called it in that great explanatory paragraph on intercession in 2 Cor. 4:7-13, "Always bearing about in the body the dying of the Lord Jesus" and "we which live are always delivered unto death for Jesus sake". This is not to be confused, as many do confuse it, with the once-for-all identification we have had with Christ crucified and risen, and we with Him, where it is said, we died, we were buried, we rose with Him. That is past and never repeated. That was His cross and resurrection we participated in for our own redemption.

What we are now talking about is not the cross for our redemption, but for the redemption of others. This is adulthood, not adolescence. This kind of cross is constantly repeated in our daily lives whenever we are in situations which our human selves would be rid of; but instead of remaining in hurt self, we recognize them to be part of some redemptive purpose of God through us in others. So, Paul says, we accept them as something we have been "delivered unto", and our "dying" which is said to be the dying of the Lord Jesus in us is our heart acceptance of them, though that may not be lightly, or easily, any more than the Savior could accept His cross without a Gethsemane.

Here is a principle of constant "dyings", daily maybe, affecting every kind of normal situation in life, not by any means in what we might call our religious activity. Anything which hurts, disturbs our *status quo*, or challenges, be it what we may call small in our personal lives, or big in some public affair, is a place of dying when we change from self's resistance to acceptance as a step in God's saving plans.

Without such dyings, Moses could never have seen that he was not to be a possible, ephemeral Pharaoh, but a savior of God's chosen people: Gideon could never have changed from challenging God's apparent indifference to accepting the challenge to be himself the deliverer. Abraham could never have exchanged his laughter at the idea of a couple of their age having a son for a productive faith. David could never have resisted the chance of killing Saul to wait in patience for God's day of his coronation. So through every aspect of achieving or enduring faith in all history. Everyone had to start by a disturbed, resisting self which saw God in the tough situation and then died to his self-resistance.

Then comes the resurrection—which is the Spirit in us causing us to see things from His point of view. We can begin to be intercessors. We can see what God is after, and the first effect is a joy, release, sense of adventure, praise where there seems nothing to praise for, for we now see the redemptive purposes, something by us for others. Its immediate effect, as Paul says, is a quickening in our own selves: "the life of Jesus manifest in our mortal flesh": burdens, fears, the sense of a hurtful, not joyful cross, is gone, and others watching can see a release and ease which is not what the world experiences in its tough spots. Resurrection life is manifested in our mortal bodies, and that by itself is God coming through us to others.

CHAPTER 19

Supercharged Action

THE REAL PURPOSE can now be discerned. An intercessor is God's strategist. He sees what God is after and goes along with Him. The men of the Bible always understood their specific commission. So must we. Any of us in any kind of circumstances can draw aside with God and examine before Him the whys and wherefores of what is happening. It will not take long before we begin to see clearly: it is for this to happen to these folks in my home, or for this in my Sunday School class or church, or to some areas of need in my city, or right out on some distant mission field. But it is specific. It is God saying to me (or to a group of us in something together), "*You* have been put by Me to stand in that gap. See that you carry it out."

I well remember how clearly, soon after my conversion, just before World War I when I had received my commission to join the regiment as a 2nd Lieutenant, the Spirit of God was wrestling with me about my affection for an unsaved girl and telling me I could not have Christ and Antichrist in my heart at the same time. There was self blocking the vision all right! The battle was won the day I took the train to our training center, and clear as daylight in that railway compartment an inner word was spoken to me, though I was the youngest of untaught Christians in those days. It said, "You are joining your regiment.

You will train for a year and then get out in the trenches. Many of you will be dead in a year. You make sure that some of those other fellows receive the gift of eternal life you now have." I couldn't "see" that great commission, until the self-block was out and I had died; but then I knew with no uncertainty my real commission within my King's commission for the next five years of war, and it became my absorbing objective to carry it out.

Later, at Cambridge University for a post-war period, once again the commission came clear (we ex-soldiers were given very easy and short ways of getting the degrees we were going out for before the war): "Whatever degree you get or don't get, you will fail at the University if you don't get souls." And once again, by God's enabling and not without often reluctant obedience, it was carried out.

These are only illustrations of the certain fact that just as every redeemed person is by that same token a priest and intercessor, so everyone who sees the meaning of self-dying to our normal self reactions in our daily lives, can hear, find, and move in on God's specific commission to them. And, of course, with mainline commissions there are always many and variable, even daily, local commissions.

With the commission comes action. An intercessor accepts the full meaning of a commission—that it is God's declared intention to fulfil some saving purpose by him, and that everything he has and is, is going into it. No one is more active than he—call him God's soldier, God's servant, God's husbandman, God's athlete. Let us make no mistake—activity, not passivity, marks him for what he is. "A body hast thou prepared me", he says with Jesus.

My own life has been spent in a missionary crusade, so I can draw my illustrations most easily from it; but that must not give any misleading idea that a foreign missionary is some very holy or very special kind of servant of Jesus Christ. You don't think that for long if you are one, or live among them! They are the most ordinary humans, just seeking to answer what they understand to be the call of God to them, not any different from any housewife or businessman who equally seeks to answer what he understands to be his call. But I have seen by them for over forty years what dedicated action means. There is a goal to be reached: it is going to be reached.

C. T. Studd, my father-in-law, went to the Congo. As a young man, when England's greatest cricketer, he had heard God's call to take Christ to inland China. He went, exchanging cricket field for mission field. In China, inheriting from his father what might be a quarter of a million dollars in today's values, he heard God's call to sell all that he had for the spread of the Gospel. He did it.

Back in England twenty-five years later, with broken health and his wife an invalid, he heard God's call to go to the heart of Africa. Against the advice of doctors, with empty pockets, called a fanatic by his friends, he went. He said, "If the young men won't go, perhaps if an old one goes and dies, they may make his grave a stepping stone and go." He lived in the Congo forests for sixteen years, while his wife by faith got off her sick bed to call recruits to join him. When he saw the crowds that poured out of the villages to greet him, he said, "Here is my black gold. They shall hear and hear to purpose that Christ died to save them." They heard, and a short while after his death, twelve thousand Africans from fifteen tribes gathered at the spot where they buried him to thank God that he had brought Christ to them.

He founded the Worldwide Evangelization Crusade with the call to young men and women to follow Christ on the same principles of sacrifice and faith, so that all nations should hear. Over a thousand have followed in forty countries, and, as I have lived with them and been one of them myself for forty-five years, I know that commissioned men and women are men and woman of action. By their bodies Christ takes His gospel to every creature: some at home in the kitchen and office: some wrestling with languages and translation: some at the printing presses: many tramping the villages in remote places or visiting the longhouses up jungle rivers: others teaching school and tending the sick, and all without salary or human security, fed by the Lord through His people.

What does it all mean? Merely this—that an intercessor is a man of action. What God commissions him to do, he does with body, mind and soul, and does not stop doing. He is a man with a purpose, a man with a goal to be reached, and the word from heaven has come to him, as to Moses, Joshua, the prophets, and to Jesus Himself. "This I am going to do, and I'm going to do it by you."

Once again we say: Let no man think this refers to special activities by special people in special places. No, this word from heaven is being heard and heeded by thousands and tens of thousands of God's intercessors in all nations all the time, and being acted upon in thousands of different ways—and among them you and me. The Church of Christ is this day "terrible as an army with banners". Let us never think that, when in former days we were active for God and exhausted ourselves in good works before we knew the secret of our inner resources in Christ, therefore, there should be less activity now. No, the opposite. More activity than ever, more straight aiming than ever, because now our resources are endless. Then we only knew how to rest from our work: now we know how to rest in our work. No one can out-work, out-think, out-pray a man in whom the Spirit of God is.

CHAPTER 20

Pigmies are Giants

IT LEAVES A wholly wrong impression if we should think that outward activity has any meaning unless it is the product of inward activity. The whole point is that an intercessor is not "working for God"; he is the human means by which God is doing His own work—and that's all. The fundamental difference is between the way we "tried" to be God's servants, when we were still under the delusion that the redeemed man does God's work for Him and with His help, and the revelation now given us that we are not really we at all, but He in us that He may be He by us. We, indeed, need to have this clear deep down to the centre of our consciousness, so that our basic outlook on what we commonly call Christian service has been revolutionized; and we cannot, simply cannot, be caught up again in that frustrating, ulcer-causing, nervous-breakdown-producing rat race of "doing our best for Him".

Our calling is to activity, non-stop activity, probably more ceaseless and intense activity than in that former way; to a sacrifice that, as with C. T. Studd and so many thousands of others, may bring us the honour of empty pockets, worn-out bodies, lives laid down (and we reckon it the highest honour God could ever give a man when it was said of Jesus, "It pleased the Lord to bruise him"). All this is now God in saving

action by us, God reaching man through man. Therefore, our first form of action is always that our inner
man is rightly geared in with the Inner Man. The
intercessor is commissioned (Is. 59:16). The intercessor is involved (Is. 53:12). But all this is meaningless
unless the intercessor is also authoritative (Heb. 7:25).
This means faith in action.

It is plain enough through all the Bible that faith
is the power line. Hebrews 11 settles that—using only
that one word to account for all the achievements in
the lives of the men of God. Faith is the whole man in
action, but primarily the inner man. We must know,
therefore, how to win our battles within before waging
them without. Indeed, every battle is in fact won
from within, and the spoils of victory gathered outside.

I should look back very differently on past years if
I had not learned and applied some of these principles
of faith. I learned them largely from another great
man of God, Rees Howells of the Bible College of
Wales. For years we have practised them in our
missionary crusade, individually and in our home base
fellowships, in every conceivable kind of need, problem
and challenge. It is authority. "Concerning the work
of my hands, command ye me." How do we talk this
same language, and faith becomes substantial? As
intercessors, we are mouths without teeth, arms without
muscles, if we have all the rest, but have not the
word of authority.

The first step must be knowing the will of God.
There can be no ifs about the word of authority.
When we are sure of His will, we can be sure of our
word of faith. How can we know? For us, it necessitated
changing the start of our prayer times from talking
to God to listening to Him. If we understand that

prayer is not our bringing our needs to God, but God moving us by His Spirit to be His channels of supply (Rom. 8:26, 27), then we form the habit of finding out first what supplies He is planning to send.

It is no light decision, because once we believe God for a thing, we really believe. We should expect God to indicate His will through our minds and desires, because "we have the mind of Christ", and "it is God that worketh in us to will and to do of his good pleasure". So we must not be afraid of our thoughts and desires. If there are several of us, we consult together. Then we come to a conclusion. We may have some Scripture which confirms us, but it is a leap of faith. We say what seems to us to be God's will.

The conclusion come to by the first church at Jerusalem in a moment of crisis is an excellent standard: "It seemed good to the Holy Ghost and to us"—a nice combination of what they understood to be the mind of the Spirit coupled with their own inner convictions, and declared as a decision of faith.

Decision there must be. Faith is always an involvement, not a sitting on the fence. Faith is always a conquest of uncertainty. But the point is that we come to a conclusion, and do not leave things in the air. Faith can only be as strong as its object: if the chair we seat ourselves on is strong, the faith is strong; if the chair wobbles, the faith wobbles. But to come to a conclusion that such-and-such is the will of God involves our reputation, and that is where we stop short. That is why we do not easily believe; it is the committal of ourselves to something, and a taking of the consequences. That is why the prayer of request is easy. We then only ask, "if it be Thy will". If it does not happen, well, it was not His will, we are not involved. But if I have said something is His will, and then it fails to materialize, I appear to be the fool or false prophet.

When the decision is settled in my mind, then the final step of faith, of my human involvement, is taken. Faith declares a thing done before it is done. It "calls the things that be not as though they were". This is the crossing of the Rubicon. Prayer puts its toes in the water: faith dives in. The Bible is filled with such incidents in the lives of all the men of faith, as well as in the Savior's life.

"Shout, for the Lord hath given you the city", said Joshua to his army before Jericho. "In the morning ye shall be filled with bread", said Moses to the hungry people in the wilderness. "Ye shall not need to fight in this battle. Set yourselves, stand still and see the salvation of the Lord", said the prophet to King Jehoshophat. "There shall be no loss of life among you, but of the ship", said the prisoner Paul to his guards on board ship at the height of the fourteen days' storm. "There shall be neither dew nor rain, but according to my word", said Elijah to Ahab.

The reason why this is possible is because prayer and faith are not our seeking to get God interested in something, but God getting us into action. Life is He in His love-activities. It is He who has put us into this specific situation; therefore, we know He has a purpose in it. We have taken time to seek to interpret His purpose and to state to ourselves what seems to be His will.

Moreover, we regard time from a different perspective. Time is a human convenience for pinpointing a fragment of eternity. We may say it is 10.00 a.m. on January 4th. But the Bible says that in eternity there "shall be time no longer" (Rev. 10:6), for God is timeless. He knows "the end from the beginning" so the end is already there. The words of prophecy were often spoken in the past tense of future events. God said to Abraham, "A father of many nations have I made thee", before Isaac was born and thousands of years before we, the church in our millions, appeared on the scene as "the children of Abraham, the father of us all". When Isaiah spoke of the Savior who was to come five hundred years later, he said, "The Lord hath laid (not will lay) on him the iniquity of us all."

Therefore, when we are faced with a need, we say God has a supply He plans to give, something He intends to do, and He has put me in the place of need as His human channel. I call this the upside-downness of God—He has the supply before the need. He had fore-ordained Christ as Savior before the foundation of the world, wrote Peter. So the Savior was there before the sinners He would come to save! The first Adam was curiously spoken of by Paul as only a figure or shadow of the final Adam, "him that was to come" (Rom. 5:14), indicating that the greatest need of history, the very fall of man, was only a great pit dug to be the foundation for God's glorious building. On this basis, therefore, we can go farther in faith than saying that God is doing a thing, and we can say, "God has done it", and we are anticipating the visible manifestation of it.

One of the best statements on this in the Bible is in Mark 11:12–14 and 20–24: when Jesus said to His disciples, "Say unto this mountain, be thou removed and be thou cast into the sea . . .". We "say" it, because "whatsoever ye desire, when ye pray, believe that ye receive them, and ye shall have them"; and the word "receive" in the original is in the aorist tense, which means "that ye received them then and there". On that basis we state a thing to be so. Thinking about a thing is non-committal, saying is a committal.

An architect may have many thoughts: his plan is his word; he is committed. We may have many thoughts or desires, or make many appeals in prayer: all are non-committal. The *word* of faith is committal. This is the critical act, and the authoritative act.

We say in faith, "God has done so and so". We demonstrate our faith by giving thanks. We are acting as kings according to the statement that we are "a royal priesthood", "kings and priests unto God". Kings speak the word of authority, "Let so and so be done". Paul said we are enthroned with Christ, "made to sit in the heavenly places with him", and, therefore, authorized and entitled to dispense His resources in His name. So we speak the word of authority, boldly acting as His mouthpiece. Prayer, which starts with asking, ends in declaring. "Thou shalt decree a thing, and it shall be established unto thee."

Having made the declaration once, do we repeat it? Continually, in the sense of thanking for what is coming. To go back to asking would be dishonest. If I have received by faith, I have received, and the proof of my having done so is constant thankfulness. But because I am a human in a human situation, I am meant to feel the pressure of things: therefore, if it is a great need, a life that desperately needs changing, for instance, I will be continually feeling the concern and burden; but I find my relief in the praise of faith, not in doubting prayer. Part of the answer, indeed, will be coming through my concerned attitudes, for I am God's feeling agent; but the difference will be between an attitude of negative unbelief which builds unbelief, or of positive faith which builds faith.

Doubts will continually recur, and unless we differentiate between the external doubts of the mind and the central faith of the heart, we get into difficulty. When Jesus said, "Whosoever shall say unto this mountain, Be thou removed . . . ", He added "and shall not doubt in his heart, but shall believe that those things which he saith shall come to pass; he shall have whatsoever he saith."

He said, "shall not doubt in his heart", not his head. There is the difference. Our reasons and emotions are what the Bible calls our soul, and they are the external means by which we express our true inner selves, which is our spirit. Our reasons express our inner knowledge; our emotions, our inner love. But both reason and emotion are open to influences from without as well as controlled from within, therefore they vary. We may think or feel one thing one moment, and another another; indeed, we are meant to, for that is our living contact with the world.

But in our spirits, our hearts, our fixed choices are made. That is where, spirit with Spirit, we are united with God. Now an act of faith is made there in our heart, our spirit. It is a free, definite, fixed choice. We have confirmed it by our word of faith. Therefore, we do not move. But doubts will recur any time. That is normal in our contact with the world of appearances, which seems to run clean contrary to faith. If we have discerned between soul and spirit, and, therefore between the variable thoughts of our minds and the invariable, fixed choices of our hearts, we shall not accept false condemnation as if we were being shaken in our faith, and mistake doubts in the mind for "doubting in the heart". We shall merely replace the doubts by the reaffirmation of the faith.

And if what we have trusted God for never seems to happen? Once we have moved over from our questionings and hesitations to what we understand to be His will and have spoken the word of faith concerning it, we never move back. It is not faith in our faith, but faith in Him. We have trusted Him. It is now His business. Leave Him to mind His own business. Even if we are tempted to think we were mistaken in our guidance, leave Him to untie the knot: He has ways in which He brings us and all concerned to the total answer: "Yes, that's it. That's what we meant by our prayer of faith." If not in time, we shall see it in eternity. He that believes in Him shall never be confounded.

There is no telling how long that will take. There is the patience of faith, the warfare of faith, the walk of faith, all of which take place, not before we have believed, but as continuance in the believing. It may be, as Isaiah said in 40:31, we start with the lofty vision and wide sweep of eagle faith; we run with the youthful vigor and enthusiasm of expectancy; we slow down to a walk, when time passes and still what we look for has not happened; but it is still the persistent walk of faith.

How many years did Noah have to keep believing, as he built his huge vessel among the critical comments and lifted eyebrows of the cynics? How many years did Abraham and Sarah wait for the promised son? For how many years did that youthful dream of Joseph's seem a ridiculous fantasy? But they each remained as fresh in faith as in those first eager days, and the proof was their immediate response of faith in action when the final summons came to take some action in the impossible.

I have found that my only real battle all the time is the inner conquest of faith. If the devil through discouraging appearances can cut my faith life-line, even for a time, I am really under the weather. Though there are many deliverances of faith thankfully to point to, there are also deliverances for which I have waited for years and not seen yet. The point is the continual repetition of the walk of faith, and a walk is step by step.

To me, to repeat again, prayer concerning such matters is never a return to asking, but a constant thankfulness that what has not yet happened visibly, has in fact happened in the invisible. Blake wrote that we are led to believe a lie, when we see *with*, not *through*, the eye. Once I have been led into a faith transaction, and the word spoken, I do not allow the devil to turn me back on myself to question my motives, as: Am I hindering God? or, Was I mistaken anyhow in my believing? No, the matter is now wholly and only in God's hands, and even if there was a mistake, or there are hindrances, I say they are "God's mistakes", and we shall see the foolishness of God wiser than men.

Inner faith, then, is the energizer of outward action. "Come now," says God, "I will do this, and I will do it through you." The two march in step in that great saying of William Carey, "Expect great things from God, and attempt great things for God."

None of us can tell in what surprising ways God may suddenly recommission us and involve us, with our hardly realizing it, in some wholly new enterprises of faith. For the Holy Spirit is at work in new ways in every generation, and we are on tiptoe for any participation in them, or for any new call to action which might come personally to us. He is always original, and may have some original calling for us. We have only to see some of His surprises today.

Who would have predicted the enormous uprise of home fellowships, like a return to church-in-the-house of the early days, where thousands upon thousands are meeting in homes for free interchange in Bible discussion, personal problems, and prayer sessions? One such movement is Faith at Work, in which I have found great inspiration by its teams of witness helping many churches to find new life on a house-group level.

Who would have guessed that the charismatic anointings of the Spirit, which, in the form of the gift of tongues has long been confined to the Pentecostals and looked on with suspicion or contempt by conservatives and liberals alike, should now have burst out and spread into all branches of the Church, and brought startling, transforming results?

It is easy to greet new movements with suspicion and to take quick note of extravagances: but I believe we, who have been settled in our faith and convinced of our right foundations, have always to be watchful lest we find ourselves to be the old wineskins that cannot stretch to contain the new wine; just as the Jews were warned by the prophets that "more would be the children of the barren than the children of the married wife"!

Who would dream that the Spirit should be at work in Rome itself, with the fresh air of honest examination, admission of errors, and opening doors leading at least to dialogue with other Christians? The right response here, I believe, is a welcoming attitude of faith and love, rather than the one that dismisses it all as a put-up job, merely a subtle way to get us all back into their fold.

There are the larger outreaches today of Christian witness, by worldwide radio, by widespread missionary activity, coupled with a growing sense of evangelistic and missionary responsibility among the younger Churches of the newly independent nations; by the great volume of Christian literature (the Christian Literature Crusade, which was born out of the World-wide Evangelization Crusade over twenty years ago, already has over 250 literature workers in more than 30 countries); by such amazing responses to the Billy Graham crusades, because Graham has been big enough to reach out and include those of all Churches as well as of none: and such movements as International Christian Leadership reaching the leadership of the United States through its Presidential, Governors and Mayors Prayer Breakfasts, and weekly prayer groups in House and Senate and many State Legislatures.

These are but a handful from hundreds of such instances of God at work today. I could fill pages with them, and probably you could too. Yet trace them down and there is the humble individual at the start, as with the I.C.L. when thirty years ago a former Norwegian immigrant, Abraham Vereide, began to see the spiritual needs of those in high places, the need of a leadership led by God, and step by obedient step God led till His witness, and those with Him, has been reaching presidents, parliament and crowned heads.

Every life is an adventure of faith, every life without exception, yours and mine: and every day has its own freshness and originality when we see it with the eyes of the intercessor.

CHAPTER 21

The Greatest Thing in the World

A ND THE LAST word—back to our beginnings—
"faith that worketh by love". If faith wins the
battles within, love wins them without. Faith in
action is love in action, and we are the eternal love.
Our active life is now lived by this new motivation.
Everything we do is part of a life of outpoured love.
That is what the Bible calls doing all in the name of
the Lord Jesus, doing it as being He doing it.

We are enthusiasts, wholehearted, thorough, because
there is a meaning to it, a purpose in it. We do not use
the word sacrifice, because love enthusiastically gives
its all to meet others' needs. It has seen and found the
great prize—the secret of the universe: to be as God
who is love. Certainly love claims all and we are the
self-given. Everything we have, everything we are, is
already given. We accept the principle of the corn of
wheat—that if it die, it brings forth much fruit. Life
for us for eternity is others living.

Does that mean years at the machine or desk or
kitchen? It may do, as the wage-earner or the housewife, in private or public life, where normal duties
fulfilled in honesty, efficiency, reliability, enthusiasm,
bear witness to a dedication beyond ourselves; and the
special opportunities arise to give the reason why:
and where love turns the fulltimer into the overtimer,

when the hours of relaxation open doors for further service.

Love knows no discrimination. Love thy neighbor, for I am to see all as Jesus Christ. Self-love has its favorites, for it is really the self it is loving, *my* parents, *my* wife, for all we really own is our self-reaction to things; that is why Jesus tells us to "hate father, mother, wife", because what we will really hate is the self-love which loves them for itself. But when the Other Self is my real self, Christ in me, then my love is self-giving and I love my loved ones for their benefit, not mine, and I love all men like that. All I still have is my self-reactions to things and people, but now they are Christ-reactions, self-giving, not self-seeking. That love possesses all. Possessiveness is to serve all, not be served by all. That love owns the world, because nothing and nobody can stop me from loving with the love which gives, not gets, and nothing is outside the reach and ownership of such love. That is God's love which owns all by giving Himself to all.

Love loves its enemies, for, as we have said, an enemy is one that wrongfully hurts me. But as I see with God's eyes I know it is not I that he has hurt, but himself. The killer kills himself, not the one he kills. So seeing with God's eyes, if a man cheats me, thinks he cleverly deceives me, robs me, I am not the cheated, deceived, robbed: he is, for he has done these things against himself. So I can love him, for I see his real need—of the Christ of God. That is how I can fulfil Jesus' words to turn the other cheek, go the second mile, give the cloak when he takes the coat. Because I can see that he is the hurt and needy one, not I, and instead of being primarily bothered by my temporary human hurt or loss, I can look to see how I can be more concerned with loving him than with my losses.

Love edifies, which means builds up. You do not build up a foundation, you build a foundation, and then build up from it. So love builds up in my brother Christian by always recognizing his foundation. When I see him, no matter how externally obscured by cloudy humanity, I see through and see Christ. There I am one with him. There I can hold to our unity when many externals of outlook, viewpoint, and behavior may separate. That is how I can be positive, not majoring on the weaknesses, but building on the fact of our one foundation.

"He that loveth not his brother whom he hath seen, how can he love God whom he has not seen?" I may have some fantastic idea of the unseen God and love my fantasy: I can see my brother as he is, no fantasy about that; and I am to love him as he is, not as I would like him to be, because I am to see deeper than the external and see the real Christ in him. I accept him as he is, and it is not for me to try to change him, but to love him as being Christ to me, and leave Christ to do the changing. In doing that I love God, for that is where God is—in my brother.

And once again, love is a debt. "Owe no man anything but to love one another." Love is ministry to others, because we love our neighbor as being ourselves. Love exists only to meet need, so love always owes because need always has a claim. Love has to pay, and the secret is that love is the eternal satisfaction, the eternal joy, the eternal freshness and gaiety, the answer to the meaning of life, for God is this eternal life and God is love.

Supposing our lives are taken from us as it has

been with some of my beloved co-workers in the Congo. That is the human ultimate of self-giving. They crowned a life spent with the Congolese, to so many of whom they brought Christ, by having their lives taken from them by some of the Congolese. What more perfect ending to the self-given life? The ending Jesus had. We congratulate them. For us it may not be martyrdom, but our lives are also given the same way. We have already died with Jesus to ourselves. We are already in resurrection life. All we have and are is no longer ours, but expendable, and we expect God to take and use it, and He does.

For a reward? Love is its own reward. It asks nothing except the privilege of loving more. That is the eternal crown. We do not look for some kind of heavenly coronation which will bring some special credit or distinction or place of prominence for ourselves, but one crowning day only—Browning's:

"So shall crown *Thee* the topmost, ineffablest,
  uttermost crown—
And thy love fill infinitude wholly, nor leave
  up nor down":

and our crown to be "like him for we shall see him as he is": and to be like Him is to be love as He is love.

So life in its fullest meaning consists of two absolutes. The first is the fact that we are not we, but He. The second, built on the first, that life is not He and we, but others.

Our final response to these absolutes is thankful recognition. We commit ourselves to Him, yes; but far more important, He has committed Himself to us, and what He takes He holds, and what He holds He moulds, and what He moulds He uses.

So we launch out into the deep of God. We launch out by recognizing that He has already seized hold of us and launched us out in His beloved Son, in whom we are and He in us. "The Lord his God is with him, and the shout of a king is among them."